THE
DEAN'S
ROLE
IN
FUND
RAISING

MARGARETE
ROONEY
HALL

The Johns Hopkins
University Press

Baltimore and

London

The Johns Hopkins University Press
2715 North Charles Street
Baltimore, Maryland 21218-4319
The Johns Hopkins Press Ltd., London

Library of Congress Cataloging-in-Publication Data

Hall, Margarete Rooney.
    The dean's role in fund raising
    / Margarete Rooney Hall.
            p.   cm.
    Includes bibliographical references.
    ISBN 0-8018-4495-9
    1. Educational fund raising. 2. Deans (Education)
3. Universities and colleges—Decentralization.
4. Universities and colleges—Administration. I. Title.
LB2335.95.H35   1992
378'.02—dc20   92-23826

A catalog record for this book is available from the
British Library.

For Russ

Contents

List of Tables and Figures   *ix*

Foreword, by Henry Rosovsky   *xi*

Preface   *xv*

Executive Summary   *xvii*

1 The Dean's Responsibility for Fund Raising   *1*

2 The Development Process   *5*

3 The Decentralization Debate   *29*

4 The Trend toward Decentralization   *37*

5 Factors Influencing AUDO Success   *43*

6 Does Decentralization Increase the Amount of Money Raised?   *47*

7 The Division of Responsibility for Development Tasks   *50*

8 Coordination and Control   *67*

9 Autonomy and the Balance of Power   *74*

10 The Management of Volunteers   *80*

11 The Flow of Communication   *82*

12 The Development Officer and the Faculty   *87*

13 The Development Officer and the University   *92*

14 Centralization: Opportunities and Challenges   *97*

15 Decentralization: Opportunities and Challenges   *101*

16 The Dean's Role in Development   *105*

Appendix 1: Survey Questionnaire   *109*

Appendix 2: Factors in AUDO Success and Division of Responsibilities: Aggregate Results and Comparison Groups   *115*

Literature Cited   *119*

Tables and Figures

Tables

1. Sample Development Positions   2
2. Contribution Goals   18
3. Types of Institutions with Academic Unit Development Officers   39
4. Age of Academic Unit Development Offices   41
5. Decentralization in Business and Engineering Colleges   42
6. Reporting and Budgeting in Decentralization   42

Figures

1. Factors in AUDO Success: Areas of Agreement   44
2. Factors in AUDO Success: Areas of Disagreement   45
3. Academic Unit Gifts as a Percentage of Total University Gifts 48
4. Fund-Raising Responsibilities   52
5. Responsibilities of the Central Office   54
6. Responsibilities to be Evenly Held   55
7. Survey Respondents by Group   55
8. Responsibility for the Alumni Database   56
9. Responsibility for Gift Records   57
10. Responsibility for Identifying Prospects   58
11. Responsibility for the Annual Fund   59
12. Responsibility for Major Gifts   60
13. Responsibility for Setting Fund-raising Priorities   61
14. Responsibility for Stewardship   62
15. Responsibility for the Case Statement   64
16. Responsibility for Proposal Preparation   65

Tables and Figures

17. Tracking Development Activities   72

18. The Effect of Decentralization on the Dean's Power   79

19. Development Officers as a Source of Internal Information   83

20. Development Officers as a Source of External Information   84

21. Assessment of Upward and Downward Communication
     within the System   85

22. Assessment of Relationship between Development Officers
     and Faculty   88

Foreword

ACADEMIC ADMINISTRATION is not an exact science; it is an art form that exhibits many eccentricities. For example, large institutions must be managed without a clearly identifiable "bottom line"; the equivalent of middle managers are the tenured faculty, none of whom can be discharged except in extraordinary circumstances; decisions that in business are normally the uncontested prerogative of senior executives, in universities are likely to be the subject of endless debates involving faculty, students, alumni, trustees, and, not infrequently, the press.

There is, however, one oddity associated with the management of higher education that strikes me at once as most important and all too frequently ignored: Top academic administrators often assume their posts with minimal or nonexistent previous experience. Quite a few academics have *started* their administrative careers as faculty deans, provosts, and even as presidents—a practice that would be inconceivable in business, where great emphasis is placed on gradually acquiring the skills necessary to lead enterprises.

Why academics seem unconcerned about proven administrative skills and whether or not this is a reasonable attitude is a complex matter. This is not the place to explore the issue in detail, but two points should be made. First, it is not unusual for a new administrator to be unaware of some of the fundamental aspects of his or her responsibilities. Second, it is extremely difficult for a person in such an unenviable position to find useful literature. Far too many books about higher education are philosophical and abstract; far too few are conceptual as well as practical. And that brings me to Margarete Hall's highly useful and most welcome volume on deaning and fund raising—a combination that is every bit as natural as ham and eggs.

My own service as dean of Harvard's Faculty of Arts and Science—I served for twelve years—greatly increased my capacity to appreciate Dr. Hall's book. Assuming responsibility for Harvard's largest faculty was my first major administrative post. All of a sudden, I found myself responsible for nearly nine thousand students, about one thousand faculty members, and a budget of many hundreds of millions of dollars. I had virtually no management experience, there were no useful books to provide guidance, and—as happens so often—my predecessor had left town and was not expected to return for at least a year. It took me quite a while to find my bearings, and I am certain that the quality of early decisions would have been vastly improved had *The Dean's Role in Fund Raising,* and similar books on equally important subjects, been available.

In American higher education there are few subjects that rank far ahead of fund raising. I say that seriously and without apology. Private philanthropy—on behalf of private and public institutions—is one of the glories of the American way of life. Today, a disproportionate share of the world's finest universities are located in the United States, and there can be no doubt that private philanthropy is one important explanatory factor. Endowments, annual giving, foundation grants, capital campaigns—singly or collectively—frequently make the crucial difference between innovation and stagnation. This applies with nearly equal force to Stanford and Yale and to the Universities of California and Wisconsin. Surely no wise administrator or academic entrepreneur will approach Dr. Hall's subject with lack of interest.

Reading this book is a very rewarding experience. The tone and topics are practical, major alternative forms of organization are covered, empirical evidence is presented, and the level of analysis can accommodate a great variety of institutions. In studying this volume, a new dean or provost will quickly understand what organizational choices need to be made and how efficient implementation should proceed. A veteran administrator will find *The Dean's Role in Fund Raising* to be an excellent account of the state of the art and a useful review of practice and procedure.

There is one thing that Dr. Hall does not say explicitly, although I think that she will not disagree with my opinion. In academic life, it is the custom to complain loudly about administrative assignments. Nearly all deans and presidents routinely claim that their greatest yearning is for the classroom and the library, and only an over-developed sense of duty and self-sacrifice keeps them from fleeing their managerial assignments. It is especially good form to complain about the yoke of fund raising that allegedly turns administrators into beggars—unwelcome visitors nearly everywhere.

Those of us who are veterans know that such a picture is carefully constructed and self-servingly false. Fund raising is fun, and many of us have come to enjoy the game. Most donors treat institutions and their representatives with love and respect, and more often than not, donors are interesting people with valuable insights. There is also considerable value in testing one's ideas with people outside your institution; fund raising gave me the opportunity to learn about my own institution while making many friends. Like everyone else, I encountered my share of no's delivered with varying degrees of emotion, but no one ever threw me out of their office or home. In general, I would have to say that alumni and other potential donors treat deans with greater courtesy than do professors or students. I recall my fund-raising adventures with pleasure and a certain amount of nostalgia. Readers of Dr. Hall's manual should know that her book is an introduction to a highly satisfying and particularly American activity.

Henry Rosovsky
Geyser University Professor
Harvard University

Preface

THIS BOOK is written for deans. It unabashedly conveys my belief that deans should have their own development officers to provide full-time, professionally competent development staffing. It talks about what deans need to do to meet their increasingly important responsibility for fund raising.

My interest in the decentralization of development activities grew from my experience in university development, first at the central level and then at the academic unit level. After several years as director of donor research and director of foundation relations in the development office of a university's central administration, I became the director of development for a college on the university's flagship campus. I was the first director of development at any of the campus's academic units; all the other development officers worked for the vice president for development of the campus and were located in the main administration building. Within a few years, several of the other deans had development officers for their colleges.

I began to take both a practical and a scholarly interest in how deans and vice presidents for development create a system that best attracts private support for the university and for the dean's academic unit. When both the central development office and an academic unit are actively involved with donors and potential donors, I wondered, how can they complement each other's work rather than diminishing each other's activities? What factors influence the success of an academic unit development office? How can the dean and the vice president for university development logically and effectively divide the development tasks so that the central office takes responsibility for those development tasks that it is best suited to handle and the dean's office takes responsibility for those tasks that are better handled in the dean's office?

I wondered what questions deans should ask themselves about the structure of their own development offices and how they should organize their relationships with the university's overall central development office. I wondered how communication should be organized, how much coordination is necessary, and to what degree contact with potential donors needs to be centrally managed. I wondered how deans could best obtain the senior staff support they need to meet their responsibilities as fund raisers.

My studies of the management of higher education grew from these pragmatic questions, which arose during the daily work of the development office and from my observations of the interactions among the people on campus who were engaged in fund raising. Studying management questions meant stepping back from development work to consider the conceptual framework within which development operates. The development office is the point of intersection between donors and the universities. Because of the impact that donors and their gifts have on higher education, development is a crucial factor in university *management.*

With this book I hope to contribute to the theoretical understanding of higher education by examining the patterns of management at various universities and comparing the outcomes of the various patterns in areas such as coordination and control, communication, and balance of power within the university and between the university and its donors. I also hope to contribute to the practice of good management by identifying advantages and disadvantages of the various patterns for managing development activities and suggesting methods for achieving success in each. I hope you enjoy reading the book and find it useful.

Executive Summary

Higher education has always sought and received private support, and recently this effort has become increasingly decentralized at research universities. Now, not only do institutions have vice presidents for development who are charged with increasing the philanthropic support of the institution, but deans are required to seek private support for their colleges within those universities.

When they are appointed, few deans have development experience, or even adequate knowledge of the theory and practice of successful development operations. Deans come from the professorial ranks, occasionally from the ranks of extraordinary practitioners. In neither case is it likely that their previous success prepared them adequately to orchestrate a successful development program.

Deans rely in part on the university's development staff to assist them. Some deans hire their own development officers to provide the expert staff assistance needed to

- define a vision for the future and plan its implementation
- build the organizational fund-raising infrastructure
- involve potential donors in the work of the college
- set goals and ask for gifts
- demonstrate the yield on philanthropic investment

Some universities continue to manage the development function centrally. In a centralized system, all development officers work for the vice president. Other systems are decentralized, with deans hiring their own development officers. In a third model, hybrid systems, there are development officers for the colleges (often referred to in this book as academic units because the word *college* excludes other units headed by deans), and their supervision is shared between the deans and the vice president.

A 1989 study indicated that many universities were decentralizing their development systems. The study identified specific management issues related to decentralization of the management of development activities, determined the importance of each issue to academic and advancement executives, and assessed the relative advantages and disadvantages of the various patterns of managing development activities.

Where decentralization occurs—that is, where the college has its own development officer—deans can take specific actions to make their development activities productive and successful. For example, deans can make sure that they are readily available to the academic unit's development officer and that the development officer interacts regularly with the faculty. They can integrate their development officers into the academic unit's leadership team. They can arrange for the academic unit's development officer to work closely with its volunteer board of advisors.

Some academic unit development officers (AUDOs) believe that success is also enhanced when the academic unit development officer reports directly to the dean, is paid by the dean, and has an office at the college rather than at the university's central development office. Chief university development officers (CUDOs) disagree on these latter three points.

When decentralization occurs, the specific development tasks and responsibilities must be divided between the academic unit and the central development office. Academic unit development officers and chief university development officers agree that the central development office should be primarily responsible for some development tasks, such as recordkeeping and acknowledging gifts. The two groups of development officers disagree strongly on the assignment of other tasks and responsibilities, particularly, soliciting major gifts, setting fund-raising priorities, and preparing the case statement.

Likewise, there is agreement and disagreement related to the issues of coordination and control of the university's fund-raising efforts. In the study, deans and vice presidents expressed some disagreement about the importance of control, although all agreed that coordination is needed. Particularly with reference to coordination, communication issues imposed themselves. Academic unit development officers believed that communication from the colleges to the central development about donors and potential donors was adequate but that inadequate information came to them from the central office. The central development officers believed the opposite.

At two levels, the study addressed the effect of decentralization on the university's autonomy. It showed that decentralization is seen as changing the balance of power on campus and that it may affect the university's ability to set its own priorities. Deans need to be aware of the power of gifts to change university priorities, and they need to remain alert to the positive and negative effects of such changes.

In summary, centralized systems for managing development meet the needs of the vice president for development better than they meet those of the deans. The primary advantage of centralization is that it provides strong coordination and control. The primary disadvantage is that it fails to fully involve the deans in the fund-raising process.

Decentralized systems, whether hybrid or fully decentralized, meet the needs of the deans more completely than they meet the needs of vice presidents for development. The primary advantage of decentralization is that it provides the deans with incentive and staffing for fund raising. The primary disadvantage is that it often fails to provide adequate coordination or control.

The deans' leadership in development must be both pragmatic and philosophical. Pragmatic leadership will assure that any of the three systems for managing fund raising will increase the support the college receives for its work. Philosophical leadership will make it clear that gifts to higher education are an investment. The return on philanthropic investment is the transmission to the next generation of the accumulated knowledge of all who came before.

THE
DEAN'S
ROLE
IN
FUND
RAISING

1 | The Dean's Responsibility for Fund Raising

TODAY'S DEAN SHOULDERS A RESPONSIBILITY for fund raising that in the past only a president assumed. Patterns of development activity in the dean's office of a large university echo the patterns of development activity seen only in the president's office of earlier colleges and universities.

Higher education has always sought and received private support. But now, in addition to colleges and universities seeking support, subunits of many colleges and universities have begun to undertake their own advancement activities. These fund raising activities can be separate from and competitive with development activities of the institution as a whole. Not only does each institution have a vice president for development charged with increasing the philanthropic support of the institution, but one or more of the deans or departmental leaders also may have a development officer who raises money to support that one college or department within the university.

Development activities of higher education have grown to be a major part of the administrative work of most educational institutions. For the academic year that ended in June 1990, the Council for Aid to Education (CFAE) reported that total voluntary support of American higher education rose to $9.8 billion, an increase of 10 percent from the previous year (CFAE, 1991). For the most part those gifts resulted from specific and formal requests for support that were planned and managed by the development officers of the recipient institutions.

There is a trend toward assigning specific fund-raising responsibilities to university deans. Thirty-five percent of the fifty-five position announcements for deanships that appeared in the *Chronicle of Higher Education* in February 1991 listed expectations related to increasing private support for the academic unit. (Table 1 presents a

Table 1: Sample Development Positions

Dean, Dedman College, Southern Methodist University
It is desired that the candidate also show evidence of fund-raising interest and ability

Dean, College of Business Administration, California State University, San Marcos
Candidates should have strong interpersonal and communication skills and a demonstrated ability to attract external funding and support for the college

Dean, Graduate School and Research Services, McNeese State University
Duties will include establishing liaison between the university and state and national funding sources; and stimulating development and submission of grant proposals and procurement of grants

Dean, College of Engineering, University of Southwestern Louisiana
The applicant should have a significant record of success in fund raising

Dean, School of Architecture and Environmental Design, California Polytechnic State Institute
Also, the dean will be active in seeking supplemental support for both new and existing programs. Also required is a demonstrated ability to develop external support and financial resources

Dean, School of Business Administration, St. Bonaventure University
Candidates should also possess the ability to foster relationships with the corporate community and alumni

Dean, Graduate School of Management and Urban Policy, New School for Social Research
Among the desired qualifications for candidates are administrative and fund-raising experience

---

Table 1 *(continued)*

Dean, College of Commerce and Industry, University of Wyoming

Major external emphases of the position are increasing the level of external funding for the college, dealing with important constituencies

Dean, College of Business, Arizona State University

Strong ties to the business community are reinforced through the existence of college outreach efforts, such as the Dean's Council of One Hundred and the Economic Club of Phoenix

Dean, School of Health, Education, and Recreation-Leisure Studies, San Francisco State University

The dean has full authority and responsibility for fund-raising programs, grant acquisitions, outreach, and public relations

Dean, College of Arts and Sciences, Texas Tech University

Specific responsibilities include research support, fund raising

---

sampling of these announcements.) In the same month five years earlier, only 12 percent of the fifty announced positions for deans required fund-raising expertise. In February 1981, only 8 percent of the thirty-eight position announcements had similar requirements.

When they are appointed, few deans have development experience or adequate knowledge of the theories or practices of successful development operations. Deans come from the professorial ranks, occasionally from the ranks of extraordinary practitioners. In neither case is it likely that their previous success prepared them adequately to orchestrate a successful development program.

Deans rely in part on the university's development staff to assist them. But the development staff cannot substitute for the deans' own personal involvement with potential donors. This has been true of presidents since the early history of American higher education. One president, John Witherspoon, who assumed the presidency of the College of New Jersey in 1770, spent most of the first year in office touring the colonies in search of contributions to support the school. He talked about specific needs of the school and of his personal commitment to it. He pointed out that "the short lives of the former Presidents have been by many attributed to their excessive labours, which it is hoped will be an argument with the humane and generous to lend their help in promoting so noble a design" (Curti and Nash, 1965, p. 36). No doubt, many deans have had similar thoughts.

In striving to meet the institutionally and personally imposed responsibility for obtaining adequate resources for their colleges, deans now spend a significant amount of their time with donors and potential donors. In some cases, the deans hire a senior development professional whose primary responsibility is to provide leadership and support to the development efforts of that specific academic unit. Such decentralization of development is not uncommon. Neither are debates about it among academic and advancement officers.

This book intends to assist deans in meeting their development responsibilities by providing ideas and information about the development process and alternative systems for managing development programs. The following chapters will

- quantify the decentralization trend and identify advantages and disadvantages of centralized and decentralized managerial systems for development
- specify factors that affect the success of academic unit development efforts
- identify areas that should always be managed centrally and those that might be decentralized
- explore the impact of decentralization on management issues such as coordination and control, communication, the balance of power, and the interaction between faculty and the development officers.

2 | *The Development Process*

THE DEVELOPMENT PROCESS is composed of five segments that have a circular relationship with one another.

Defining a Vision for the Future and Planning for Its Implementation

The dean's most important development responsibility is to formulate an inspiring academic vision for the college, even if that vision must be based on downsizing rather than on expansion. The vision leads logically, although often not easily, to an implementation plan that is the foundation of an effective development process.

Donors want to invest their scarce philanthropic resources where the return on their investment will be greatest. In other words, they want their gifts to make a difference. A clearly articulated plan of action leading to the implementation of an inspiring goal shows potential donors the projected impact of their gifts.

The dean should know where the college has been, where it is now, and where it will be in a few years. The dean should identify past and current successes of the college and use them as a foundation for an action plan leading to specific future achievements. The college's leadership group can then articulate and implement programs that will transform the actual into the visionary. No single document can be written to direct the transformation. The vision will inform and support all decision making. It will be the standard against which activities and programs are measured. The dean's vision of the future of the college unifies all of the planning and implementation activities.

A senior development officer can be an important contributor to this leadership group. A visionary goal draws the college toward change. Change affects the use of and need for resources. Each member of the college's leadership group brings some resources to the discussion of how to achieve the goal. The development expert brings an ambitious and aggressive evaluation of the ability of the college to attract private support for reaching its goal. Others bring ideas on reallocation of current human and financial resources and on the initiation of nonphilanthropic resource-enhancing programs, such as noncredit courses that return more revenue than they expend or programs to produce patentable materials. Together, the college's leaders set realistic objectives that are the framework for their implementation activities.

These dynamic planning sessions are not limited to meetings where planning is the primary agenda item. Because the goal becomes part of the leadership's group culture, planning is part of every leadership meeting, formal or informal. Without the participation of a development expert, a college tends to fall into the trap of accepting a goal, envisioning programs and activities that would achieve the goal, estimating the resources needed for implementation, projecting the resources that will be available from current known sources, and assigning the development office to fill any gap.

With an expert advancement officer as a member of the team, the group can include objectives that will involve potential donors in goal-oriented activities and enhance the amount of philanthropic support that will be available. The team can realistically assess the time and money that the college is willing to expend on development activities and the resources that can be attracted from philanthropic sources. The likely outcomes of the development process can be included in the overall evaluation of resources available for implementing the academic plan. If, after the development process has been included as a planning factor, a gap exists between needs and resources, the management team will be in a position to adjust the implementation plan or its time-line in order to address the gap. A management process that integrates development leads to enhanced success.

The dean who knows what the college's role has been in the past, what it is now, and where he or she is leading it can be inspiring and practical in describing the impact of donor investment in the college.

It is helpful to create a list of indicators of the college's past and current productivity and success. Because each audience measures success differently, the list should include the following items to help various people and groups understand the impact of the organization:

- *student data,* including number of applicants, number served (both majors and those attracted by the curriculum and teaching reputation despite their unrelated majors), SAT scores, GPAs, comments on student evaluations

- *faculty data,* including academic credentials, peer recognition, community involvement, comments on student evaluations

- *alumni data,* including number, anecdotal evidence of success, satisfaction rating on alumni surveys, participation as donors, participation in alumni activities, participation in student recruitment programs

- *program data,* including ratings by media, grantmakers, or other outside evaluators of the college or of component programs and curricula, and anecdotal evidence provided by corporate recruiters, employers of alumni, parents, and students

In an eloquent description of basic human aspirations, Si Seymour, an early leader in the development profession, said that everyone wants to be pursued and everyone wants to be a worthwhile member of a worthwhile group (Seymour, 1988, p. 6). By combining a clear vision for the future with indicators of current and past success, the dean defines the college as a worthwhile group. By specifying the impact that contributions will have in continuing current success and enabling the implementation of the vision, the dean defines the donor as a valued participant in the group, a full partner in its achievements.

Building the Organizational Fund-raising Infrastructure

The dean will always be the chief development officer of the college. Position descriptions now make this fact clear by specifying that expectation. To be successful in attracting private support for the college, the dean must have senior staff advice and assistance, influential and affluent volunteers, and a systematic process for identifying prospective donors, keeping records, acknowledging gifts, and assuring that the donors' designations are followed.

Staffing

Attention may be the primary ingredient in success. The dean needs a good development officer who will attend to fund raising full time and focus the dean's full attention on it at the most important times. A senior development officer will help the dean identify the indicators of organizational excellence, find the right words and images to convey a clear understanding of the vision to various categories of potential donors, and implement the development process.

The dean needs to find a development professional who will serve as a trusted, inner-circle advisor, one of the key members of the administrative cabinet. If the development officer is a member of the central development staff, rather than the dean's staff, the college will lose the benefit of full development participation in planning. Development officers from a centralized development office seldom meet the college's needs as well as development officers based in the academic unit.

Advocate-Volunteers

The dean must build a circle of influential and affluent advocates. These advocates may form an advisory board visitors. (I advise against calling the group the board of advisors unless you, as dean, really want their advice. If given the title "advisors," they may offer counsel in areas such as curriculum or faculty development where it is not fully appropriate.) The advocates may be the members of the university's high-level donor recognition group, often called the President's Club, who have an academic or philanthropic affiliation with the college, or they may be a small and informal cluster of individuals who care about the dean's plans for the college's future and want to help.

Strengthening and nurturing this group is an ongoing process. The development officer must devote a great deal of attention to showing these advocates how their participation is vital to the success of the college. To keep them involved, the dean must give the advocates achievable and helpful tasks to accomplish.

Identifying Potential Donors

The college must identify potential donors. The dean will need to be involved personally in the identification process and will also rely on assistance from the college's or central administration's development staff.

The prospects will be businesses, foundations, and individuals.

PROSPECTIVE BUSINESS DONORS

There are several reasons for a business to become a college donor. If the college adds to the body of knowledge (by developing or evaluating technological or managerial programs or processes) that the business uses to increase profitability, giving is a matter of enlightened self-interest. It is also in the best interest of the business to support the college if the college provides the business with employees. Not only do businesses want to be favored recruiters but they want the college to have the resources to provide students with a strong learning experience so that the students will be better prepared for the workplace. There will also be businesses who give because of the advocacy of one or more of the college's influential supporters. Knowing these donor motivations helps to identify potential donors and to decide which of them deserves early and intensive attention.

Companies that have consulting arrangements with faculty may be prospective donors because the college is providing them with needed expertise. Additionally, through the faculty consultants, the college has advocates within the company. Companies whose work relates to areas of college research expertise are also potential donors. The prominence of the college's research expertise, the proximity of the company to the campus, and the profitability of the firm are also considerations.

The dean should identify other potential business donors by reviewing the list of corporate recruiters who visit campus specifically to interview graduates of the college. Those firms employing the college's alumni can be identified through current records, by having an alumni directory prepared, and by talking to those who are active in the university's alumni activities and association. There is no direct cost to the university for having such a directory prepared. Several companies provide this service in return for authorization to market the directory.[1]

1. The membership of the Counsel for the Advancement and Support of Education (CASE) includes many organizations and firms that provide services in the areas of publications, public relations, fund raising, and alumni relations. Check

Higher education contributes greatly to the well-being of a region. An educationally rich region provides its businesses with well-prepared employees, and it helps businesses to recruit top employees who often place high value on the educational and cultural opportunities available to themselves and their families. Higher education provides cultural and recreational activities that add to the vitality of a region, enhancing the economic health of a community as a major consumer and employer. Business thrives in a thriving environment. For these additional reasons, giving to a college is a wise business investment.

PROSPECTIVE FOUNDATION DONORS

Many corporations establish corporate foundations either to move the grant-making an arm's length from the operation of business or to help make the grant process more professional. Identifying foundation donors requires an understanding of the varying types of foundations, of which corporate foundations are one. Although the management of the corporate foundation is distinct from the operational or executive management of the company, the motivations for giving are the same. Corporate foundations like the Mobil Foundation, the Sears Roebuck Foundation, or the AT&T Foundation give to help meet a need of the corporation, such as those already discussed for well-prepared employees and an economically healthy region. They give in the company's self-interest.

National foundations, like the W. K. Kellogg Foundation, the A. W. Mellon Foundation, or the Ford Foundation, are another type of foundation, with different goals. They seek grant recipients who can help them achieve their goals, which often involve solving societal problems. Foundation publications and reports in specialist newspapers and magazines will help to identify those few occasions when the college's expertise and objectives will overlap with the goals of a national foundation. Only when there are overlapping goals does a national foundation become a realistic potential donor for the college.

Regional and community foundations specify that all recipients must be located in a certain geographical area. A review of the published materials from each of these foundations will identify those

the CASE membership directory, surely available from your campus development office, for names of companies that produce alumni directories.

few that are potential donors to the college. Most states maintain a list of all foundations, and the list should be available through the attorney general's office or a library. The Foundation Center is a national resource library maintained by contributions from foundations. In New York City, Washington, Cleveland, and San Francisco, the Foundation Center provides a wide range of services. In about one hundred other cities, it has affiliated collections that have information on all foundations.[2]

Family foundations are essentially mechanisms for wealthy individuals. They seldom have professional staffs or published materials, and they often respond less than promptly to inquiries. They are listed in state directories of foundations and are included in Foundation Center files. Because their principals are essentially distributing money earned by themselves or their families (unlike foundations with program officers, for whom providing grants is a profession), these foundations should be cultivated with the same techniques employed for individuals rather than those used for organizations.

The impact of a corporate or foundation grant is greater than its dollar value. A corporate or foundation grant implies competitive selection and endorsement of the quality of the college by the foundation or corporation. Taking note of this can be helpful in future fund raising as well as other advocacy activities.

PROSPECTIVE INDIVIDUAL DONORS

Most private support comes from individuals, not from corporations and foundations. Therefore, most of the college's efforts should focus on identifying prospective individual donors. Review the list of past donors, looking for people who might be able to give more for the current appeal than they gave in past years. Ask senior faculty members to do the same and to suggest names of alumni who they believe could give if motivated to do so. Ask active alumni to identify prominent and successful classmates. Have the alumni list electronically screened by one of the several firms that will rank lists for their giving potential, using techniques developed by marketing

2. More information about the Foundation Center's locations and services is available by calling 1-800-424-9836.

firms.[3] Ask upper-level donors to identify other alumni and non-alumni who might give at a comparable level or higher.

Rank the potential donors according to their capacity to give and their inclination to give. For example, alumni with abundant family wealth and seven-figure annual salaries reported by the media should probably have an A+ ranking for capacity. If they have had no contact with the campus since graduation, the ranking for inclination should be much lower, perhaps a C–. Taken together, these rankings will assist in setting a priority for your cultivation and solicitation activities.

Recordkeeping and Stewardship

The quality of recordkeeping and gift management will directly affect the success of the development program. Donors deserve timely and appropriate acknowledgement of their investment in the college and in the dean's vision of a better future. The ability to deliver a brighter tomorrow loses credibility if the college does not successfully deliver a gift receipt.

Donors often make their gifts in pledges for contribution over a specified period of time. Therefore, a pledge-reminder system is essential. One of the maxims of the fund-raising profession is that **no one ever gives without being asked.** A pledge is a sign of good faith on the part of the donor that he or she will still want to be part of your work in the future. The donor deserves the courtesy of a request for the gift.

Assuring that the donor's gift is used for the purpose specified can be time-consuming and difficult. The more gifts that are raised, the more complex the stewardship issues. Scholarship administration is particularly prone to slipping from the donor's designated uses. Because the financial aid office, the accounting office, and an academic office are jointly involved in the awarding of each scholarship, many opportunities for error exist. For example, a donor may have requested that a committee of faculty select potential recipients for the scholarship and allow the donor to have some input in the selection process.[4] After the donor comments, a final choice must be made by the

3. The CASE membership directory can provide the names of some of the firms that do electronic screening.

4. The donor cannot, however, be the selecting official. If the donor retains

campus's selecting official. When the student is informed, the financial aid office must be told and must take action to inform the accounting office that the student's fees will be partially or fully covered by the award. The student accounts office must make it happen. To assure that any gift is used as intended, an efficient system is needed from the point at which someone remembers to set up the faculty committee, to the point at which the student's fees are paid, and, perhaps, the student pens a note of appreciation to the donor.

Although in complex universities, records and stewardship are the primary responsibility of people outside the college, the dean's reputation and ability to succeed in fund raising are at stake regardless of whether the stewardship responsibility rests directly, or only indirectly, with the dean. The dean should assure that processes are in place to acknowledge and record gifts, to administer scholarships and grants, and to keep the dean informed through both formal and informal networks. The responsibility for these very important development activities is often shared between the central development office and the college. The dean should assure that each group knows what it must do.

The dean may also want to review the language used to thank donors and to request contributions toward their pledges. Often when the pledge reminders or gift receipts are generated by a computerized system, they have been written by people more familiar with billing language than gift language. The dean will not want the college's donors to be thanked for, or asked to send, their *payments.* The donors should be thanked for, or reminded to contribute, their *gifts.* A donor to a small, liberal arts college in Maryland once wrote across a poorly worded pledge reminder that he "surely had no *payment due* to the college. If the president wanted a gift from him, he would have to ask for a gift, not send a bill." The development office discarded its stock of remaining pledge reminder forms and printed more appropriate ones.

In addition to the receipt and reminder system that is in place in the central office, the dean should establish a system for thanking major donors to the college. Coordinated duplication will be an indication of the importance of the donor's gift. In addition to the stew-

---

control over the specific use of the money, then he or she did not fully give it away and no gift can be claimed for tax purposes.

ardship system that is in place to manage the use of gifts, the dean should create a backup system to assure that the most important donors receive reports demonstrating the impact of their contributions.

In summary, the infrastructure of the development program will require

- top-tier professional staffing for the dean's efforts
- influential and affluent volunteer advocates
- ongoing research to identify and rank potential donors
- accurate and sensitive recordkeeping, pledge management, and gift stewardship

Involving Potential Donors in the Work of the College

All prospective donors are not equal and should not be treated equally. Working with a senior development officer, the dean should segment the potential donors according to the size of the gift each might make. The pool of potential donors will include individuals, businesses, foundations, and organizations. When sorted according to the size of a likely gift, the donors will form a pyramid with a broad base of individuals and organizations, probably included by category rather than listed by name. For example, the base might include

- alumni who have never made a gift
- alumni with less than $250 in accumulated giving
- parents of current students
- regional companies that do not recruit on campus
- regional foundations with assets of less than $5 million

Above the base will be a sizeable number of potential donors of midrange gifts. These will be companies, foundations, organizations, and individuals with more money and, therefore, more ability to give, if they were motivated to do so. They will probably not give at their maximum potential initially. These donors will also include people and organizations that are likely to give if asked but that do not have the capability to give a very big gift. These potential donors should be identified by name.

At the narrow top of the pyramid will be a few potential donors who can make very large gifts to the college. They will be identified by name and might include very successful, or very lucky, alumni or a profitable firm that regularly hires students from the college.

Strategies for involving potential donors in the work of the college will differ with their position on this prospect pyramid. The small number of prospects at the top are the most important to fund-raising success. Their gifts will probably result in 90 percent of the gift revenue. They deserve at least 50 percent of the dean's fund-raising attention.

Another fund-raising maxim is that **people give to people.** Therefore, it is essential that prospective donors of major gifts become familiar with the leaders, faculty, and students of the college. Some of the potential major donors will be individuals whose gifts come from their personal wealth, others will be organizational representatives whose gifts come from their company's or foundation's wealth. Regardless of whose money is involved, the personal involvement of the decision-maker with the dean and the college is a key to the success of any development program.

Some particularly effective volunteer tasks put the potential donors in direct contact with the students. For example, one business college asked corporate leaders to judge a day-long competition in which student teams planned and presented business strategies. The competition was the final exercise in the students' capstone course designed to integrate all the information from their other business courses and focus it on solving problems. The corporate executives evaluated all the students, not just the best ones. This gave them a real feeling for the quality of the college's program. They knew that the event was not a contrived showcase for the college but, rather, an integral part of the curriculum. They saw that their participation enhanced the value of the experience for the students. The companies represented on those panels almost always became regular, major donors.

Another way to involve potential donors is for the dean to annually invite key donors and some potential donors to volunteer to participate in a planning and evaluation retreat. An effective technique is to hold the retreat at the home of a wealthy donor where casual dress is encouraged and where the office will seem pleasantly remote. Structured and unstructured discussions will flow on topics related to the college's current and planned programs and to the environment in which the college's students will find themselves after graduation.

The particular interests of individual participants will become clear. New interests will emerge. Donors and potential donors will be reconfirmed in their commitment to the college's goals, in their confidence in the college's management, and in their decision to give generously.

A third way to involve potential donors is for the dean to identify four or five current high-level donors who are willing to assist the college. The dean would ask each of them to host a breakfast or dinner at which the dean would talk about the college and his or her vision for its future. Each volunteer then would identify about five people to come to the event; the development officer could usually add one or two to each list. The volunteer would call to issue an invitation, saying something like: "I would like you to come to my office for breakfast next Friday and meet the dean of the College of Arts and Sciences at Regional University. I am a donor to the college and think it is important to all of us. I would like you to meet the dean."

At the breakfast the dean would make a presentation. The host would remind the guests of the importance of support and would ask the development officer to call each of them soon. The guests could be given a packet of information about the college. The development person would do the rest. This is very effective, high-level cultivation. The potential donors would already have been identified as capable of top-tier giving. They have been invited by a person whom they know and trust to be a good judge of the value of the college. And, they meet the dean. Such events usually result in about half of the participants making gifts at the targeted level.

There are too few hours in a day to give adequate attention to all potential donors. The amount of time spent cultivating a potential donor should correspond to the donor's potential level of giving. (Of course, if such advice were followed strictly, it would mean that low-level donors would seldom be given any attention. And, yet, low-level donors are important too, for they provide the base from which major donors rise as individuals' disposable incomes rise. Therefore, the rank-and-file donors also need to be cultivated.) Because 90 percent of the gift revenue will come from the few donors at the top of the giving pyramid, the dean must concentrate on these donors.

Setting Goals and Asking for Gifts

Goals

The dean should set two types of goals for the college's fund-raising efforts: activity goals and dollar goals. The activity goals should specify how many donors will be identified at the midrange and upper levels of the pyramid of potential gifts. (A rule of thumb is that you will need to identify four prospective donors for each needed gift.) The activity goals should specify the number of visits and other cultivation meetings to be completed, the number of major proposals to be submitted, and measurable actions to be taken to report to donors on the impact of their gifts. For example, the activities goals might be the following:

1. Identify 20 prospective donors for 6-figure gifts, 40 prospective donors for 5-figure gifts, and 200 prospective donors for 4-figure gifts.

2. Complete 100 cultivation/involvement events (personal meetings, campus visits, Board participation) between potential major donors and the president, the dean, a volunteer/advocate, or the senior development officer.

3. Submit 40 proposals for gifts of $10,000 or more.

4. Send each major donor an annual report showing how the contribution was used and what impact it produced, and send each donor of $100 or more a thank-you letter from the dean within two weeks of receipt of the gift and an annual listing of all donors with a brief report on how private support was used to enhance the quality of the college.

Dollar goals should specify both the amount of the contributions to be received during the year and the amount of the pledges to be received for future contributions. Especially when the dean is initiating a new development office, pledges are important. They demonstrate the strength of the dean's program and the level of support. Pledges also provide a base for the coming years, so that the dean's efforts build from a higher starting point in subsequent years. Dollar goals that fit with the activity goals shown above might look like those in Table 2. Dollar goals must relate directly to the prospect

Table 2: Contribution Goals (in dollars)

Designation	Pledges	Gifts	Total
Unrestricted	50,000	250,000	300,000
Programs	200,000	150,000	350,000
Scholarships	250,000	250,000	500,000
Endowment	250,000	150,000	400,000
Total	750,000	800,000	1,550,000

identification and cultivation activities. The need for resources and the goal for fund raising are seldom identical. As mentioned earlier, colleges sometimes err in goal-setting by assuming that the fund-raising goal is the difference between the amount needed to operate the desired programs and that amount available from less fungible sources. Such faulty thinking leads to disappointed advocates, angry faculty, and frustrated deans.[5]

Good management and a good product are prerequisites for obtaining revenue, regardless of the source. Building a donor base and increasing the revenues from private gifts require planning, time for cultivation, and effective solicitation. There are few "untapped sources" simply waiting like maple trees for a passing dean to poke them with a spigot and draw off the disposable income. Perhaps even more than taxpayers or tuition payers, donors need to be convinced that their investments in the college will yield valuable returns. Because these returns to them will be intangible, however, convincing them will not be easy.

The goal for fund raising should be set after studying the number of potential donors, evaluating the likelihood of changing them from potential to actual donors, and deciding the level at which each can realistically be expected to give. Fund raising is a process; it is not magic. The college cannot hire a magician to meet unrealistic goals based on wishful program planning. Instead, there must be a process of thoughtful and ambitious prospect evaluation.

5. For more on goal-setting, see Duronio and Loessin, 1991; Lees, 1986; Seymour, 1988; and Smith, 1981.

Asking for Gifts

THE CASE STATEMENT

Because there are many worthwhile organizations seeking contributions and because donors are becoming quite sophisticated about their philanthropic investments, the dean, development officers, and advocate-volunteers must be able to make a strong case for giving to the college. The fact that the college does important work and does it well is not likely to be adequate. Some organizations develop an entitlement attitude that is self-defeating. Consciously or subconsciously, these organizations appear to be saying that potential donors owe them contributions because they are working at below-standard salaries in less-than-ideal conditions. There are many organizations that need support. Donors seem to prefer the ones that make them feel that they are participating in good works, rather than merely compensating an organization.

The dean should develop a case statement, which is a statement of the reasons for supporting the college. (Case statements are sometimes developed into publications, but, often, they are simply shared with staff and advocates as a means of assuring continuity in the message to the outside world.) The dean should make sure that the case statement focuses on the potential donor, not on the potential recipient. The reason for giving is not that the college has legitimate needs but, rather, that society has real needs and that the college, in partnership with its donors, can address those needs effectively. The case statement could include

- a statement of the societal problem that the college addresses
- a statement of the college's approach to solving the problem
- indicators of the college's past and current success
- an overview of goals
- an outline of measurable objectives to move the college toward its goals
- a projection of costs and revenues

Above all, however, the case statement should provide the summary rationale for a gift to your college. For example, the basic tenet of the case for giving to the Big College of Arts and Sciences at Very Big State

University may be that the college graduates five thousand students a year, 60 percent of whom stay in the region. Inevitably, graduates of the college will make up the economic, social, and cultural backbone of the community. A gift to the college is a direct investment in the future of the region.

On another hand, the foundation of the case for giving to Not Very Big College of Fine Arts at Quality First Private University may be that the college provides a unique asset that attracts to the community unusually talented individuals with remarkable leadership strengths. People who place special value on proximity to fine arts, and the companies these people lead, will seek and accept jobs in the region because they enjoy proximity to the college and its community services. A gift to the college is an indirect investment in the economic and social vitality of the community and a direct investment in its reputation as a dynamic cultural center.

With a basic statement formulated, the dean can enhance the case and shape it to fit the need for an unrestricted gift of support to the college or to fit any proposal for programmatic support. All of the dean's fund-raising work will be rooted in the basic case statement.

MAJOR GIFTS

The actual solicitation of gifts from those individuals at the top of the gift pyramid will be relatively easy. Having identified these potential donors, set a cultivation and involvement strategy for each of them, and implemented that plan, the dean and the development officer will know these prospects well. The dean's volunteer advocates may know them even better. The potential donors will be so involved with the college that the dean or an advocate can easily go to them to discuss a gift.

Another fund-raising maxim is that **a gift results when the right person asks for the right gift at the right time.** The right person may be one of the dean's advocates whom the potential donor respects. The advocate must have already made a contribution and the contribution must be at least as much as the one being requested. The only exception is when the advocate and the prospective donor have greatly differing degrees of wealth. If the advocate knows the prospective donor well enough and has enough influence on the prospective donor to be the right person to ask for the gift, the advocate and donor will have comparable ability to contribute. If the solicitor is Mother Theresa, for example, she may be effective in asking for a gift larger than her own, but only because her smaller gift represents a philanthropic commitment comparable to the larger gift by the wealthier donor.

The right person to ask for a gift may be the dean or the development officer. However, if they do ask, they, too, should be donors. The right person to ask may be a business peer, whose endorsement would bring credibility to the college and influence other potential donors. Selecting the right person to ask for the gift is an important part of any fund-raising process.

The cultivation and involvement process will also have helped determine the right amount to request of a donor. Previous and current donors can be asked to upgrade the level of their support. With them the dean has a place to start. But the prospect identification process and conversations with individuals during the cultivation process will have produced data to confirm the early estimate of where they should fit on the donor pyramid. Remember that a donor is seldom angered by being asked for too much. Many prospective donors are even flattered that the college officers believe they're capable of making such a large gift. Because almost no one ever gives more than requested, it is almost always best to err on the high side.

Major donors deserve to be asked for their gifts in person. The dean and the senior development officer can form a good team for such solicitations. However, an even better team may be the dean, the senior development officer, and a volunteer-advocate. They can all talk about the proposed use of the contribution and its impact in the area of the potential donor's interest. Any one of them can request that the prospective donor consider a gift to support this area of interest. A specific gift amount should be suggested and it should be clear to the prospective donor that all members of the team are supporting the project as well.

The solicitation should occur after the prospective donor has become involved with the college, but it is not necessary to wait until the prospective donor seems to have adopted the organization as a primary philanthropy. Being solicited may help the prospective donor realize how important the gift could be to the college. Even a negative response can be a step toward a positive response the next time the prospective donor is asked. A positive response is almost always the first step toward the next solicitation. Giving is a very important cultivation tool. Because a major donor has a vested interest in the college's continued success, he or she is very likely to continue giving. No major donor wants to admit that a gift was a mistake—making another gift is even preferable to admitting the first one went to an unworthy organization. In a sense, you almost have to drive a major donor away.

For major donors, particularly for corporations and foundations, the college should prepare a formal proposal requesting a contribution. The proposal is often a follow-up to a face-to-face meeting with the potential donor, at which time the potential gift was discussed. The proposal can either be a short letter or several pages long. Foundations often specify the length and, sometimes, the format of a proposal. The materials that help to identify a foundation as a prospective donor to the college will give these requirements.

Although their preferences differ as to format and length, all foundation officers appreciate brevity and clarity. Because the proposal or letter will be read by only one person at a time, the dean should make sure that any request going over his or her signature is addressed to a single person. Below are a few points to consider:

1. The title of the proposal should describe the desired results, not the activity to be undertaken. For example, "Improving Emergency Responses of Latchkey Kids" is better than "A proposal for a classroom module on use of 911 numbers."

2. The table of contents in a longer proposal will act as an outline and an overview. It should highlight the most important aspects of the proposal.

3. An abstract, useful in a longer proposal, should put forward only the bare essentials of the problem, solution, expertise, and cost.

4. The statement of the problem must be clear. The problem will relate to the basic case for giving to the college. It should, like the case for giving, be bigger than the organization and should relate directly both to the potential donor's interests and the college's goals and expertise. One example: The problem in the example given above is not that the college needs to release a professor from

teaching one course for one semester in order provide time for writing a series of new curriculum modules. The problem is that more than 25 percent of children let themselves into homes and are without adult supervision for more than 30 minutes after school each day. These children need additional training on safety issues and on wise use of community assistance resources. A second example: The problem is not that the College of Education needs to renovate its classroom space but that American children are failing to achieve their full potential in school. At least part of the reason for this is that teacher education programs are not preparing classroom teachers to use available technology. It takes more than putting computers in classrooms to improve education. Classroom teachers have to be prepared to use technology as an integral part of the curriculum. Future teachers need to learn the technology in school themselves. While handling all their classroom duties and having to prepare six or more fascinating and motivational lesson plans per day for each of three or more achievement levels of students, new teachers cannot be expected to create ways to use the computer, investigate available software, or figure out what is the best way to use the technology with children at one achievement level and then modify it to be equally effective with children at a different achievement level. Finding a way to prepare teachers during their teacher preparation program is an important national issue.

5. The goal should be stated in global terms, as the title given above is stated. The objectives should be specific and measurable. If the goal is to improve emergency response in latchkey kids, the objectives might include producing a comic book that shows how to use 911 emergency systems or developing a crew of children to write and produce a video for local cable showing how to handle a stranger who comes to the door. If the goal is to increase the use of available technological innovation in traditional core curricula, the objectives might include the enhancement of ten classrooms to provide state-of-the-art hardware and software for teacher preparation classes.

6. The procedures should specify the steps that will lead to the achievement of the objectives. How will the children who will do

the filming be identified? Where will the project leaders get the needed equipment? Who will train the children? Or, who will identify the appropriate hardware and software to be installed in the new classrooms? Include information about the college's expertise, the timetable, and evaluation and dissemination plans.

7. The budget should show all costs and revenues, not just those requested of this prospective donor.

8. An appendix might include letters of endorsement from prestigious leaders and current students.

9. A cover letter can relate this project to the overall vision for the future of the college and stress the priority given to the project.

After having submitted a proposal, keep the prospective donor informed of activities at the college. Materials sent while a proposal is under consideration are likely to be kept with the college's file and may help to give the prospective donor a more clear picture of the value of the proposed project.

MIDLEVEL GIFTS

Midlevel gifts can often be very successfully solicited by your advocate-volunteers. This process becomes a cultivation tool for the solicitors as well as a solicitation technique. The solicitors are brought together for an orientation or provided with orientation materials. They are given a script that helps them to internalize the case for giving. They are asked to make their own gift before asking others. It is difficult to organize the number of volunteers needed for midlevel personal solicitations, but it is usually very successful when done well. If the college has few midlevel volunteers, it may be advisable to forego this technique in favor of a mail campaign.

DIRECT MAIL

Direct mail is expensive, difficult, and much less productive than personal solicitation. However, it does permit the college to reach a larger audience and acquire new base-level donors who can then be cultivated for future upgrading to higher levels of giving.

Obtaining a mailing list of alumni names and addresses from the university's records system is sometimes difficult. Alumni mailing list problems are only the beginning of the challenges of conducting a direct mail appeal. If foundations, organizations, companies, or non-alumni such as parents or community leaders are included, mailing lists must be developed from sources other than the university's records. The lists must then be maintained and updated.

The college's solicitations will need to be coordinated with other university solicitations. Text must be written and letters must be produced either by word processor or at a print shop. A carrier envelope, reply card, and return envelope must be designed and printed. The whole set must then be folded, and the envelopes must be stuffed, stamped, and packaged in accordance with complex postal regulations.

Someone must decide whether or not to personalize the letters. If they are personalized, salutations must be examined carefully. The person who signs the letters must make sure that she or he is not addressing a neighbor or former classmate as Mr. Smith when Bob is appropriate. In addition, reply cards must be matched to the letters, so that Mr. Smith's letter does not include a reply card with Mr. Jones's name and identification number on it.

Letters should be targeted to the recipients. Previous donors should not receive the same letter as nondonors. Those who have given at the same level for several years should be asked to consider upgrading to the next level.

Many firms will handle direct mail for a college. It may be wise to have a direct mail house handle the more complex and technical tasks.[6] Sometimes the university can provide services through a central print shop to coordinate at least the printing, folding, stuffing, stamping, and mailing.

If the objective is to raise as much money as possible for the college's programs, it is more effective to ask a few prospective donors for big gifts than to expend the time, money, and energy asking many prospective donors for small gifts. Proper identification of the giving capability of the prospective donors will make it as easy to obtain a $50,000 from a wealthy person as to obtain $50 from a person of

6. Almost every community will have firms that provide direct mail assistance. Some will specialize in nonprofit direct mail and have experience with agencies providing social service, with hospitals, or with environmental organizations. You could contact leaders of those kinds of organizations for a recommendation of a mail firm or mail house. The CASE membership directory or the membership directory of the National Society of Fund Raising Executives (NSFRE) can lead you to some service providers. For information, call NSFRE at 1-703-684-0410.

modest means. The rule of thumb is that it requires four prospective donors for each gift; that is to say, three people will say no for each one who says yes. To raise the $50,000, therefore, the college must identify, cultivate, and solicit four people who could give the whole amount, or it must write and produce four thousand letters to people who could give $50 each and are motivated to do so by their previous involvement in college activities. With an eye on the gift pyramid, direct-mail fund raising is a good use of time only after major-gift fund raising is well under way.

For soliciting the rank-and-file donors and acquiring new donors, phonathons are an alternative to direct-mail fund raising. A return of 5 percent on direct mailing is considered good. A phonathon may bring a 20 percent return or better. But phonathons, do have many challenges. The primary challenge among them is retaining a volunteer calling team. Because people have come to greatly resent the intrusion of phone solicitations into their private time, those called often vent their resentment on the callers. Using paid student callers increases the cost but lessens the difficulty of recruiting callers. This also makes it possible to require training, regular attendance, and help with paper work. Phonathons do not eliminate the need for sending letters, for a mailed piece must follow the phone contact. In addition, it is necessary to get phone numbers and to print caller information cards showing past giving records and other information about the potential donor's involvement with the organization for the callers to use.

There is so much planning, detailed preparation, and follow-up demanded in order to have a successful direct mail and phonathon effort (combined with the low results in revenues raised by these efforts compared to major gift activities) that it is very tempting to encourage the central development office to take responsibility for this task, thereby allowing the deans to use their time cultivating potential major donors. If any deans are at the beginning of a fund-raising effort for their college, I encourage them to use their time primarily on major donor activities and to let the central development staff handle the donor acquisition through direct mail and phonathons.

In summary, the dean needs to set goals and ask for gifts. The preparation of a case statement will help to confirm the college's goals and objectives and to demonstrate its achievements and expertise. Personal solicitations by the dean and advocate-volunteers, with staff support from a senior development officer, will follow logically and naturally on the activities undertaken to involve prospective donors in the real work of the college. Written proposals finalize and specify the earlier discussions between the potential donor and the dean. Direct mail and phonathons are costly in time and money, and often they are best handled by the central development office.

Demonstrating the Yield on Philanthropic Investment

Gifts to higher education are as much an investment as the dollars put into business, real estate, or retirement portfolios. But the return on philanthropic investments is more important than the return on other investments. The return on gifts to colleges and universities is the transmission of shared knowledge and values to the next generation. The dean must assure that gifts are used as the donors intended them to be used, and the dean should convey that assurance to the donors. Integrity is a key ingredient in long-term success of the college's development program.

As stewards of philanthropic investments, colleges owe donors an honest view of the impact of their generosity. The dean should regularly and clearly communicate to the donors how their gifts made a difference in peoples' lives. The dean should strive to give donors a fair share of the sense of achievement that the college staff gets from working with students.

With the help of the college's or the central administration's development officers, the dean should provide individual reports to major donors showing the impact of their gifts. These will usually be letters reporting on how their contribution was used and what resulted from the support given. For some donors, such a letter can be very effective when done informally with homey comments from the dean about the impact of the gift. For others, a formal report is preferable. If the contribution supported a program, results of the program can be described. If it supported research, outcomes can be discussed. If the contribution supported a scholarship, information can be shared about who received the support and how well the student has progressed toward graduation. In addition to an acknowledgement letter at the time of the gift, all donors should receive an annual listing of donors to the college that shows the impact of their accumulated generosity. Major donors should also receive a report when their contribution has been used and annual interim reports if the gift supports multi-year activity.

Good stewardship is the best possible preparation for the next solicitation.

3 | *The Decentralization Debate*

Conflicting Responsibilities

Deans and vice presidents for development do not always coexist peacefully. The official expectation that deans can and will raise private money to help their academic units excel overlaps with the formal assignment to vice presidents of the responsibility to plan and implement university-wide development programs.

Disagreement between deans and vice presidents often begins with the discussion of "who's in charge here?" It continues through "who understands best where the alumni place their allegiance?" and "who can respond most effectively to the needs of the alumni and other constituencies?" and it is headed for real trouble when it reaches the debate about "who didn't give whom the information about the most recent contact with the prospective major donor?"

The disagreements reflect real dilemmas. Which development tasks are best handled by the central development office and which by the academic units? Is loyalty to the whole university a stronger or a weaker motivator for philanthropic giving than loyalty to the professional program from which the alumnus or alumna graduated? Does the need for university-wide coordination and control of development activities interfere with the need for deans to have ownership of their own development programs?

Definitions

Important distinctions differentiate centralized and decentralized systems for managing development activities. In a decentralized system, the dean hires development officers to raise money designated to support the academic unit. By contrast, in a centralized system, the vice president hires development officers to raise money for the whole university. In a centralized system, responsibilities are usually divided by the type of donor, that is, the Director of the Annual Fund, the Director of Corporate Relations, or the Director of Foundation Relations. These central development officers often raise money for individual academic units, but no central development officer has an academic unit as his or her primary fund raising focus.

Hybrid systems also exist. In this book, a system is considered hybrid, or semi-decentralized, if there is a development officer whose primary responsibility is to raise money for an academic unit but who is paid, at least in part, by the vice president.

The Roots of Centralization

Although many university deans and a minority of development experts favor decentralization of the development function, the bias of a majority of experienced development officers and some deans is toward centralization. The bias has many credible and influential parents, including the history, tradition, and the experience of successful past fund raisers.

The battle to bring the development function into the mainstream of higher education management was hard fought and only fairly recently won. The establishment of central development offices headed by vice presidents signaled that universities had accepted development as a full partner in managing higher education. Decentralization is perceived by many academic leaders and advancement officers as a retreat from the commitment to development's role as one of the key functions of high-level university leadership.

Development activities are as old as higher education in America. "After erecting shelter, a house of worship, and the framework of government, one of the next things we longed for and looked after was to advance Learning and perpetuate it to Posterity. . . . And then, it would seem, almost as a matter of course, there was Harvard" (Rudolph, 1962, pp. 3–4). Early colleges were meant to instill loyalty, citizenship, and order, and to train clergy and teachers for the next generation (Rudolph, 1962). Colleges were founded to bring civilization and Christianity to the wilderness and to train a "learned leadership" for the future of the communities (Curti and Nash, 1965, p. 3). "The size of the continent, religious differences, and rivalries among the colonies" led to a proliferation of institutions (Curti and Nash, 1965, p. 22).

Efforts to obtain adequate resources to maintain the colleges began with the very first institutions. There were nine colleges in the colonies. The presidents of the institutions were in constant search of adequate funding to maintain them. It is thought that Nathaniel Eaton, the first master of the college founded at Newtowne in the Massachusetts Bay Colony, brought John Harvard, a fellow Cambridge University man, to visit the new school and influenced him to leave half of his estate for its support.

The succeeding president of Harvard College is known to have hired agents to return to the mother country and solicit gifts for the school. The agents were armed with a brochure, *New England's First Fruits,* describing the college and its goals and vision of the future.

Colonial governments provided some support for William and Mary, Harvard, Yale, and King's College, but colleges for the most part relied on private resources (Curti and Nash, 1965, pp. 22–23). During the period between the Revolution and the Civil War, the states had few resources to invest in higher education. Denominationalism accounted for the establishment of many new colleges, each supported primarily by a religious faction (Rudolph, 1962, p. 55). Over time, colleges were founded to educate students in more practical fields, to offer education for women and black people, and to provide graduate education. Even when states again became more involved in supporting colleges and universities, acquisition of private support remained important to most institutions.

Then, as now, the efforts to obtain private support were led by the institutions' presidents. Although almost every college hired agents to seek private support, these fund raisers remained outsiders and were not part of the institutional leadership. Early presidents were not able to rely solely on these external solicitors.

Presidents had an essential role in cultivating philanthropists' interests in their institutions. For example, Mark Hopkins, president of Williams College, received a benefaction in the 1840s from Amos Lawrence, a wealthy textile manufacturer, because Lawrence liked a speech that Hopkins had given as part of the Lowell Lectures in

Boston. Hopkins nourished the interest of philanthropist Lawrence by regularly writing to him about the college and the impact that Lawrence's philanthropy was having on the institution. Lawrence is said to have cherished the esteem of Hopkins and continued his philanthropy as much out of friendship with the president as out of concern for the school (Rudolph, 1962, pp. 179–82).

As colleges became more diversified in their instruction, presidents continued to play a key role in attracting the support to expand the curriculum and to establish and maintain the newer institutions. His trust in, and respect for, zoologist and geologist Amos Eaton convinced Stephen Van Rensselaer to provide support for the establishment, in 1824, of a small institution devoted to the practical arts (Curti and Nash, 1965, p. 65). An inaugural address by Harvard's president Edward Everett in 1846, and his later efforts to provide at the school instruction in the practical sciences, inspired Abbott Lawrence to offer support for such instruction (Curti and Nash, 1965, p. 68). The ability and vision of Milo Jewett, president of Cottage Hill Seminary, confirmed Matthew Vassar in his desire to support higher education for women (Curti and Nash, 1965, pp. 92–97).

Deans have had like experiences of meeting philanthropists through their professional affiliations and as a result of speeches, writings, and presentations. The interest of these philanthropists has been nurtured through continuing communication, visits to the campus, and service on task forces or committees.

Despite the long history of philanthropic support for higher education, the role of the development officer as an integral member of the university staff and management is relatively new. Around 1900, a few colleges set up news bureaus to send information about students to their hometown newspapers. But by the mid-1940s, only a handful of institutions had fully staffed public relations offices (Reck, 1946, p. 2).

As early as 1643, the alumni of Harvard were returning to campus to renew old acquaintances. In 1821, the University of Michigan hired an alumni secretary to help alumni keep in touch with one another. Alumni of Princeton and a few other institutions gave money during the Civil War to help their institutions keep the doors open despite the turmoil and disruption (Reichley, 1978 p. 277).

But as late as 1942, fewer than half of America's colleges and universities had an alumni annual fund. In 1949, the membership directory of the American College Public Relations Association (ACPRA) first listed two individuals with the title of director of development, and in 1952 there were still only thirteen (Pray, 1981, p. 1).

In 1958, the Ford Foundation sponsored the Greenbrier Conference, at which alumni, public relations, and fund-raising officers built "a new conceptual framework" for institutional advancement. This organizational framework was "gradually adopted by the majority of institutions in the succeeding two decades" (Pray, 1981, p. 2). The conferees suggested that public relations, alumni affairs, and development be unified under one executive who would report directly to the president and be a member of the institution's top management team (Porter, 1958, pp. 57–59). "But perhaps the most challenging development has been the growing concept of fund raising and advancement as integral parts of a total organizational structure with more intimate and stronger relationships with other elements than before" (Pray, 1981, p. 5).

Many of today's senior leaders of higher education, both development officers and academic officers, participated in this centralization of the advancement functions into a new office with vice-presidential power. They reorganized their universities. They fought the necessary battles to create the central development office because they realized that having several advancement activities scattered about the campus, without high-level, central leadership, was inadequately effective. Having internalized all the strong conclusions of the Greenbrier Conference, they became fully committed to centralization of the development function.

The institutional advancement officer today plays one of the key roles in the management of higher education institutions. Most colleges and universities have executive officers who carry this responsibility. Such officers are peers of the executives in charge of administrative affairs and academic affairs. Often joined by the senior student affairs officer, these individuals are the chief institutional advisors to the president.

Because the advancement officer is the manager of the institution's efforts to secure private support, he or she stands as a bridge between the institution and its constituents. The participants in the Greenbrier Conference and other leaders of higher education successfully argued that the development officer cannot be an adjunct to the institution, but must be an integral part of it (Muller, 1978 p. 9). Advancement officers must be involved in the essential decisions that relate to the organization that they represent to the constituents, including its planning (Adams, 1978; Pickett, 1981; Muller, 1978). The development officer is responsible for communicating with both internal and external audiences. In order to communicate effectively, the officer must be a highly visible participant in the institution's top management, anchored in the core work of the institution. The Greenbrier Conference recommendations contrasted sharply with earlier assumptions that the public relations and other advancement functions were subsidiary or peripheral programs of the institution. (For more on the development officer's role in management, see Adams, 1978; Blaney, 1988; Franz, 1981; Goldman, 1988; Muller, 1978; Pickett, 1981; Reck, 1946; Rowland, 1974; Swearer, 1988.)

When the possibility of decentralizing development operations has been mentioned, decentralization has often been perceived as a throwback to the earlier fragmentation of the advancement functions. Decentralization has been seen as a withdrawal of the commitment to fully integrate the development function into university top management.

The bias favoring centralization is rooted in this history of the development function in higher education. Many senior development officers and consultants continue to favor centralization because they've seen that it has brought effectiveness and power to the development function and because they have had no experience with the new decentralization that might cause them to question their centralization bias.

A Historical Perspective on Decentralization

A vocal minority of development officers and a great many deans favor the new decentralization because their experiences convince them that fully centralized management of the development function is not always the most effective structure. Like the proponents of centralization, these decentralization advocates can cite some historical roots to their side of the debate.

Hofstader and Metzger (1955) believed that early gifts to higher education were too small to be truly influential. But during the post–Civil War era, gifts were much larger and carried greater power. New philanthropists were higher education entrepreneurs and were not accustomed to passive roles. "In the case of 90 percent of the money given to a large institution the initiative is taken by the donor, and not by the university concerned. . . . Thus big business and professors came into fateful contact. The former supported the university and took command of its organ of government, the latter surveyed society and tried to sway its course; two spheres of action and interest, formerly far apart, drew close and overlapped" (Hofstader and Metzger, 1955, pp. 140, 144).

Even if not in total agreement with Hofstader and Metzger, decentralization advocates argue that the assignment of development officers to academic units responds to the high level of involvement of philanthropists with the faculty and leadership of the academic units.

Because faculty today are often more closely affiliated with an academic unit and a dean than with the university as a whole and the president, donors who are interested in faculty-centered programs are as likely to be in contact with deans as with presidents. Deans need professional development staffing to take advantage of these gift opportunities.

In fact, some deans argue effectively that the recommendations that development professionals have used since the Greenbrier Conference to explain the need for centralizing the management of development can best explain their desire for decentralizing it. Decentralization is essential in order to assure that the development officers are part of the top management of the organizations to which the gifts are made—the academic units of the university. The deans say that development officers must not be adjuncts to their colleges. Rather, they must be involved in the essential decisions of the organizations that they represent. They are responsible for communicating with both external and internal audiences. In order to do that effectively, they must know the faculty and their research, and they must be in step with the culture of the academic unit, its alumni, and the people it serves.

This debate cannot be judged democratically. Despite the majority opinion that development should be centralized, many universities are less centralized than they previously were. The issues raised by decentralization are important both to those who are currently less than fully centralized and to those who are considering decentralization.

Evidence of Increasing Decentralization

A discussion of the decentralization of fund raising at research universities is far from a theoretical debate. A study completed in 1989 indicated that between 1985 and 1988, more than 40 percent of the 213 research and doctorate-granting universities had hired a director of development for either their business or their engineering college. It showed that another 13 percent planned to hired such an academic unit development officer by 1991. In many universities, both the dean and the vice president are said to be responsible for development. But the management system that the university has in place for the development function will give either the dean or the vice president the authority to meet that responsibility directly. The other one of them will have to meet the responsibility indirectly, either by working with or by circumventing the authority.

As the higher education enterprise has become complex and sophisticated, the trend toward decentralizing the development function has accelerated. Deans want full-time, professional assistance in meeting their development responsibilities. They believe that having such assistance will increase their fund-raising success.

4 | *The Trend toward Decentralization*

As the director of development for a business school at a research university, I began to notice that there were more people at professional meetings who had positions similar to mine. Curious as to whether decentralization was occurring at a large number of institutions or was only an anomaly at a few institutions with special, nongeneral situations, I planned a short investigation. I conducted a telephone survey in August 1987. To keep the size of the sample surveyed to a practical number and to have the units surveyed be comparable to each other, I included only two academic fields: business colleges and engineering colleges. I chose them because a study of the membership directory of the Council for the Advancement and Support of Education (CASE) indicated that they were the colleges most likely to have their own development officers.

I randomly selected one hundred colleges, fifty from among the 655 domestic educational institutions that were members of the American Assembly of Collegiate Schools of Business (AACSB) and fifty from among the 267 institutions listed in the 1986 annual report of the Accreditation Board for Engineering and Technology (ABET). All of the engineering programs that are included in the annual report are accredited by ABET, but AACSB does not accredit all of its members. Those selected from among the AACSB member colleges were representative of the membership as a whole, 37 percent of which were accredited. Forty-two percent of the random selection were accredited. Responses were received from all fifty business colleges and from forty-seven engineering colleges.

Each college was asked four questions:

1. Does your college have its own development officer separate from the university or campus development officer?

2. To whom does the development officer report?

3. Who pays the development officer?

4. How long has your college had its own development officer?

Twenty-seven percent of all the academic units I interviewed during the telephone survey had their own development officers. Moreover, 50 percent of those at research or doctorate-granting institutions did. Only one percent of those at comprehensive or liberal arts institutions had their own development officers.

Of the business schools at research and doctorate-granting universities, 57 percent reported that they had their own development officers. All of these business schools were AACSB accredited; none of the non-AACSB-accredited business schools had their own development officers. Of the engineering schools at the same type of universities, 44 percent had their own development officers.

I also learned that 56 percent of business and engineering schools that were part of public research or doctorate-granting universities had development officers, compared with only 36 percent of similarly classified colleges that were part of private universities (see Table 3).

The results made it clear that decentralization was occurring, but only at research and doctorate-granting universities, and that a lot of deans and development officers were involved in the decentralization debate. Many of those interviewed expressed a desire to learn more about how other universities were addressing the challenges and opportunities of their development programs.

I continued the study, looking only at research and doctorate-granting universities. I conducted case studies of three universities in order to identify specific management issues related to decentralization of the management of development activities, to determine the importance of each issue to academic and advancement executives, and to assess the relative advantages and disadvantages of the various patterns of managing development activities.

Each of the three universities had a Carnegie classification as a research university, and each had a business school accredited by the AACSB and an engineering school that belonged to the ABET.[7]

7. The Carnegie Foundation classifies all institutions of higher education which are listed in the *Higher Education General Information Survey of Institutional Charac-*

Table 3: Types of Institutions with Academic Unit Development Officers (in percentages)

	AUDO Status	
Institutional Characteristics	*With AUDO*	*Without AUDO*
Research and doctoral institutions	50	50
Comprehensive and liberal arts institutions	1	99
Business colleges at research and doctoral institutions	57	43
Engineering colleges at research and doctoral institutions	44	56
AACSB-accredited business colleges at research and doctoral institutions	57	43
Not AACSB-accredited business colleges at research and doctoral institutions	0	100
Public research and doctoral institutions	56	44
Private research and doctoral institutions	36	64

The pattern of managing development activities was different at each of the three universities studied. At the first institution, called Decentral University in this book, management was fully decentralized. Both the business school and the engineering school had their own development officers. Each development officer was paid from the school's budget and was supervised directly by the dean. The university also had a vice president for advancement and a central development staff reporting to him.

At the second university, called Central University in this book, management was centralized. At this institution, the business and

teristics into ten categories: Research University I, Research University II, Doctorate-granting University I, Doctorate-granting University II, Comprehensive Universities and Colleges I, Comprehensive Universities and Colleges II, Liberal Arts Colleges I, Liberal Arts Colleges II, Two-year Colleges and Institutions, and Professional Schools and Others Specialized Institutions. Classification is based on the level of degree offered and the comprehensiveness of their missions.

engineering schools had neither their own development officers nor a development officer assigned to work primarily with either school. The development officers at this university were part of a central office and worked on university-wide priorities, which included the business and engineering schools.

The third university, called Hybrid University in this book, had a hybrid system for managing development. All development officers were part of the central university development office. They were paid from the budget of the central university development office. One development officer was assigned to work with the dean of the business school and one with the dean of the engineering school. The deans and the vice president for advancement jointly selected the development officers assigned to the schools. The academic unit development officers were located in the schools and worked as staff to the deans.

At each of these three institutions, interviews ranging from thirty to sixty minutes were conducted with academic and advancement leaders, including presidents, provosts, deans, vice presidents for development, and academic unit development officers. Each interview broadly covered topics of productivity, management effectiveness, employee motivation, executive involvement, information flow, goal setting, coordination and control, prospect identification, cultivation and solicitation, and other development and management issues.

I subsequently mailed a survey to chief development officers and the directors of development of the business and engineering schools, where such positions existed, at each of the 213 research and doctorate-granting universities in the nation. Included were a total of 204 chief university development officers, or CUDOs (9 positions were vacant at the time) and 108 academic unit development officers, or AUDOs (63 business and 45 engineering). Of the 312 questionnaires mailed to 213 institutions, 202 individuals (65 percent) from 156 institutions (73 percent) responded. A copy of the questionnaire is found in Appendix 1.

Sixty-one percent of the institutions from which a response was received had either a business or an engineering development officer or both. Compare this to the 50 percent who responded to my telephone survey. This large increase probably reflects an actual growth in the number of AUDOs. In the mailed survey, I asked those who did

Table 4: Age of Academic Unit Development Offices (in percentages)

Years Academic Unit Development Office Has Existed	At Engineering Colleges	At Business Colleges	Total
< 1	13	14	14
1–3	38	30	34
4–6	23	33	28
7–9	16	10	13
> 9	10	13	12

not have an academic unit development officer if they planned to hire one soon. Thirty-four percent said they would hire one within two years. With that expectation in mind, the increase from 50 percent to 61 percent is credible. The responses to both the telephone and mailed survey also indicated that the academic unit development offices had been established recently, giving added strength to the likelihood of such a large increase.

Of the twenty-six academic units with development offices in the telephone survey, only one had established the office more than ten years earlier. Only five more had development offices that were more than five years old. The remaining twenty had hired their development officers within the previous five years and fifteen of them said they had hired their first development officer within the previous two years.

Many (48 percent) of the decentralized offices responding to the mail survey were reported to have been initiated within the previous three years. Seventy-six percent of them had existed for fewer than seven years and only 12 percent had been in place for longer than nine years (see Table 4).

Of the respondents at institutions with an engineering school, 46 percent indicated that the institution had a development officer for that school. Fifty-three percent of the respondents at institutions with a business school said that the institution had a development officer for that school (see Table 5).

Thirty-one percent of the academic unit development officers reported to their deans; 14 percent of them reported to the central de-

Table 5: Decentralization in Business and Engineering Colleges (in percentages)

	AUDO Status	
Institutional Type	*With AUDO*	*Without AUDO*
Engineering colleges in research universities	46	54
Business colleges in research universities	53	46
All research universities	61	39

Table 6: Reporting and Budgeting in Decentralization (in percentages)

Characteristic	*Business*	*Engineering*	*Total*
Report to the dean	36	24	31
Report to the vice president	11	18	14
Joint reporting	52	57	54
Paid by the dean	48	31	41
Paid by the vice president	21	34	27
Jointly paid	28	32	30
Paid by university-related foundation	na	na	3

velopment office; 54 percent of them reported jointly to the dean and the central development office.

According to the respondents to the mailed survey, the budgets of the academic units paid the salaries of their development officers in 41 percent of the cases. The salaries of the academic unit development officers were paid by the central office budgets in 27 percent of the cases. The salaries were paid jointly by the budgets of the academic units and the central development office in 30 percent of the cases. In 3 percent of cases the academic unit development officers were paid by a university-related foundation (see Table 6).

Despite the fact that decentralization advocates are a minority among advancement and academic leaders, decentralization is occurring at a rapid pace at research universities. Managing the results of the decentralization is important to success and productivity.

5 | *Factors Influencing AUDO Success*

WHERE DECENTRALIZATION OCCURS, deans can take specific actions to make their development offices more productive. The seventy-three AUDOs and sixty-eight CUDOs at decentralized and hybrid universities that responded to the survey evaluated the relative importance of the following factors in influencing success:[8]

1. Being paid by the dean
2. Reporting to the dean
3. Being physically located in the academic unit
4. Being part of the management team of the unit
5. Having easy access to the dean
6. Having a high level of interaction with the faculty
7. Having interaction with the students
8. Interacting with the academic unit's volunteer board
9. Interacting with the university's primary volunteer board
10. Having a good rapport with the university's chief development officer
11. Having a good rapport with the university's president
12. Having an academic title (assistant, associate dean)
13. Having a dean who is committed to the development effort

The development officers were asked to indicate if they considered each factor to be essential, helpful, or unimportant to AUDO success. There was a consensus on the importance of several of the factors. A majority of all the respondents taken as an aggregate, a majority of

8. The sixty-one CUDOs from centralized systems did not participate in this segment of the survey.

Figure 1. Factors in AUDO Success: Areas of Agreement

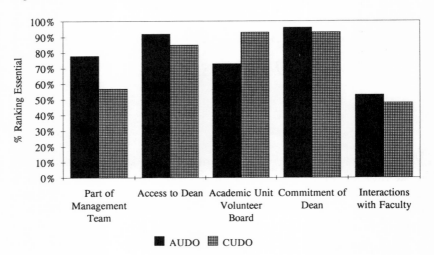

the CUDOs, and a majority of the AUDOs, agreed on the following items (see also figure 1).

1. Being part of the management team of the academic unit was essential to success. The AUDOs were most strong in this ranking, with 78 percent of them responding that it was essential. The AUDOs at fully decentralized institutions placed the most value on this factor, with 83 percent of them ranking it as essential compared to 74 percent of the AUDOs at semi–decentralized institutions. Less than 10 percent of any group ranked it as unimportant.

Like the Greenbrier Conference participants before them, today's deans and development officers understand that a development officer cannot be an agent of the college. As a bridge between the college and its external constituents, a development officer can represent the college well only as an integral member of its management.

2. There was consensus among all development officers that having easy access to the dean was essential, with at least 79 percent of each group ranking it as such.

3. The respondents were close to a majority agreement on the importance of having a high level of interaction with the faculty. In

Figure 2. Factors in AUDO Success: Areas of Disagreement

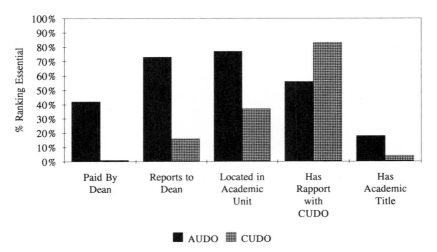

each group, about 50 percent of the respondents ranked it as essential and about 50 percent ranked it as helpful.

4. Almost 75 percent of each group ranked interacting with the academic unit's volunteer board, the board of advisors or visitors, as essential, with 93 percent of the CUDOs giving this ranking and only 73 percent of the AUDOs.

5. All groups agreed that interacting with the university's primary volunteer board, usually the board of trustees or regents, was helpful. Between 63 and 70 percent of responses in each group fell to this ranking. Of those who did not rank it as helpful, more ranked it as essential than as unimportant.

6. There was clear consensus on having a dean who is committed to the development effort. More than 90 percent of all respondents ranked it as essential and fewer than 2 percent of any group ranked it as unimportant.

Despite this agreement on many issues, AUDOs and CUDOs had significant disagreements about the importance of each of the following factors (see figure 2):

1. Most CUDOs ranked being paid by the dean as unimportant, while the rest ranked it as only helpful. Few AUDOs ranked it as

unimportant. There was also a significant difference in response between AUDOs at fully decentralized institutions and those at semi–decentralized institutions. The majority of the former ranked being paid by the dean as essential while the majority of the latter ranked it as helpful.

2. Many CUDOs ranked reporting to the dean as helpful, while almost as many ranked it as unimportant. This ranking placed them clearly apart from the AUDOs, the majority of whom ranked it as essential, with almost all of the rest ranking it as helpful. Only 4 percent of AUDOs ranked it as unimportant compared to 40 percent of the CUDOs.

3. Being located in the academic unit was given less value by CUDOs than by AUDOs. Seventy-seven percent of AUDOs ranked this location as essential, while only 37 percent of CUDOs did.

4. More than half of the respondents in each group ranked interacting with students as helpful. The other half of each group split between unimportant and essential, with more CUDOs saying unimportant and more AUDOs saying essential.

5. Although almost no one ranked having a good rapport with the chief university development officer as unimportant, there was a major difference between the percentage of AUDOs who said it was essential and the percentage of CUDOs who did. Only slightly more than half of the AUDOs (56 percent) ranked it as essential. Of the CUDOs, 83 percent gave it an essential ranking.

6. While more than half of each group ranked having a good rapport with the president as helpful, at least another quarter of each group ranked it as essential. More CUDOs (19 percent) ranked it unimportant than any other group.

7. Rankings on having an academic title differed greatly among the groups. Sixty-four percent of CUDOs ranked it as unimportant, while only 28 percent of AUDOs did. Only 4 percent of CUDOs ranked it as essential, while 18 percent of AUDOs did.

6 | *Does Decentralization Increase the Amount of Money Raised?*

THE KEY INDICATORS OF SUCCESS in development are the commitment of the chief executive officer to development activities, the financial resources allocated to the development program, and the commitment of an active trustee or volunteer group (Pickett, 1981). It is intuitively obvious that the amount raised is also likely to relate to the size of the university, its age, its geographic location, its prestige, the wealth of its primary constituency, and the degree to which its research has industrial implications. Changing the management structure of the development office is only one of the many factors that may affect success. Development is a snowball crashing down a hill. It is hard to start the action, but once it is started it has its own momentum. All of these factors taken together determine the degree of incline of the development hill. Most of them the dean cannot change. Therefore, it is tempting to try the few changes that are possible.

The deans who participated in the case studies were all convinced that they could raise more money for their colleges with decentralized development than with centralized development. And 88 percent of the total of 141 survey respondents at decentralized institutions said that the establishment of an academic unit development office led to an increase in philanthropic support of their universities. With these two indicators of faith in the efficacy of decentralization, in 1991 I conducted a third survey in conjunction with the Clearinghouse for Research on Fund Raising at the University of Maryland. Those business and engineering schools that I knew (from the earlier survey) had AUDOs, I asked to provide data about the amount of money raised by the academic unit before and after the academic unit development office was established.

Only 8 percent of them responded with usable data. Another 4 per-

Figure 3. Academic Unit Gifts as a Percentage of Total University Gifts

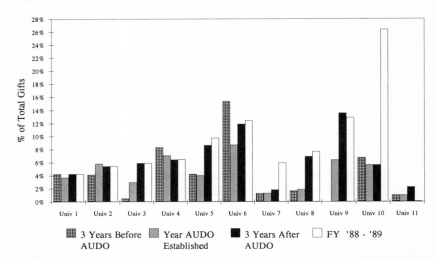

cent wrote to say that the data were not available. I suspect that the lack of response is attributable to the lack of data or the extreme difficulty of accessing the data that exist. Even the small amount of data received provided some interesting anecdotal support for the opinions expressed by the deans and development officers in the 1989 study.

Of the eleven usable sets of data, all showed that the academic unit raised more money in the three years after the establishment of an academic unit development office than in the three years before the office existed. More importantly, at six of the schools the data showed that the academic unit received a larger percentage of the total amount of private support received by the university in the years immediately after hiring the AUDO than it did in the years immediately before the change. One of the academic units received a smaller percentage immediately after the AUDO was hired, but it is now raising a much higher percentage than it did before it had an AUDO. One raised a larger percentage immediately after the AUDO was hired, but it has not maintained that high percentage. Two of the academic units raised a smaller percentage after they got an AUDO than they did before having one, and they continue to raise a smaller percentage.

To arrive at these conclusions, I took the accumulated amount raised in the two or three years (depending on the available data) before having an AUDO and compared it to the accumulated amount raised in the next two or three years. All of the academic units increased the amount raised. These accumulated amounts were then expressed as a percentage of the university's total giving in those same years in order to minimize the affect of inflation and university-wide changes in giving patterns. Although more data are needed, it appeared that having an AUDO helped 70 or 80 percent of the respondents to increase the private support for their academic units (figure 3).

7 | *The Division of Responsibility for Development Tasks*

DECENTRALIZATION RAISES THE FOLLOWING worrisome questions related to the development process:

1. How will the goals and objectives of the academic unit be integrated with those of the university when they are presented to potential donors?

2. Who will raise money for innovative programmatic needs?

3. Who will assure that nonprogrammatic institutional needs, such as scholarships and faculty enhancement, are met?

4. Who will raise money for the annual operating budget? for the capital fund? for endowment?

5. Who will identify prospective donors?

6. Who will decide which potential donor is a prospect for which project?

7. Who will assure that all of the constituents, including the parents, students, nonalumni friends, faculty, and staff as well as the alumni and corporations and foundations are given the opportunity to make a philanthropic investment in the university?

8. How will the decentralized system avoid ignoring constituents like parents or current students, for whom data is not usually easily accessible?

9. How will the decentralized system avoid sending inappropriate duplicative solicitations to the constituents who overlap between academic units, such as alumni with an undergraduate degree in one area and a graduate degree in another, parents of more than one student, or businesses interested in several areas of university expertise?

10. Who will record the gifts?

11. Who will send pledge reminders?

12. Who will report to donors on the use of their contributions?

The institution must decide how these operational functions will be handled. When an academic unit establishes its own development operation, none of the functions can be overlooked. Either they all must be achieved by the academic unit development office or a clear division of responsibility for them must be established between the central institutional development office and the academic unit development office.

The following are among the more important tasks that the development process must accomplish:

- setting fund-raising priorities
- preparing the case statement
- maintaining alumni databases
- identifying prospects
- conducting the annual fund
- managing a major individual gifts program
- managing a major foundation gifts program
- managing a major corporate gifts program
- preparing proposals
- maintaining gift records
- assuring gift stewardship

The tasks are often achieved through the joint efforts of the central development office and the academic unit development offices, but the responsibility for assuring that each task is accomplished must be clearly assigned. Furthermore, the division of responsibilities is likely to differ during a Capital Campaign and during times of routine fund raising.[9] I asked the surveyed development officers whether the re-

9. A Capital Campaign is an intensive, special fund-raising technique that has a limited time frame of two to five years, identifies a number of specific fund-raising priorities (often physical facilities or endowment) and relies on the involvement of an affluent and influential committee of volunteers. A Capital Campaign usually occurs in addition to, not instead of, routine fund raising. One incomplete, but usefully brief, comparison of routine fund raising and Capital Campaign fund raising claims that the former seeks recurring gifts from disposable income for

Figure 4. Fund-Raising Responsibilities (aggregate group assignment)

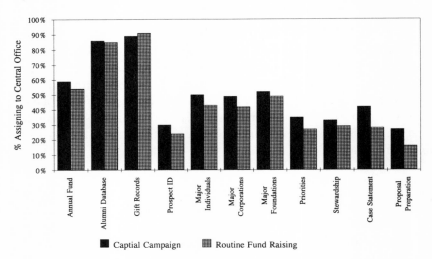

sponsibility for each of these tasks, during a Campaign and during the routine development process, should be assigned primarily to the academic unit, to the central development office, or evenly held by the academic unit and the central development office. They often tended slightly toward centralization when the university was in a Campaign. Compare the task assignments in figure 4.

The tendency to move away from centralization during non-Campaign fund raising is particularly pertinent because the development world is probably entering a new cycle. For several years now, everyone has been in a Campaign. Major Capital Campaigns tend to be university-wide events designed to unify the campus and all of its constituents, focusing everyone's attention on obtaining the resources to achieve a significant new level of academic excellence. Some recent Campaigns have been extraordinarily ambitious, with goals exceeding $250 million. A few institutions have undertaken Campaigns with goals exceeding $1 billion. A university that is not planning for, executing, or just completing a Campaign has been considered unsophisticated in its development operation.

recurring university needs. The latter seeks one-time gifts from the donor's equity assets for the university's physical plant or endowment assets.

Donor burnout, administration exhaustion, and the recessionary status of the economy have come together to end this cycle. Over the next decade, universities probably will be less noisy about their development. The mega-campaigns will almost certainly give way to less ambitious projects, to fund raising on a more human scale. The pleasure of working with a group of potential donors to achieve a shared goal will replace the carnival-like kickoff dinners and black-tie extravaganzas of the recent past. Universities, donors, and society will enjoy the respite. The tendency of development officers to prefer centralization during Campaigns will be less of a factor in the decentralization debate.

Aggregate Responses

My survey showed that, when the responses were analyzed in aggregate (that is, when I did not segment the AUDOs and the CUDOs), most development professionals favored centralization. Even more of them moved toward centralization during a Capital Campaign. Given the three choices of assigning primary responsibility to the central office, or the academic unit, or having them held equally responsible, there is no area of responsibility that a *majority* of the development officers would have assigned primarily to the academic unit.

In contrast, a majority of the respondents said that, both during routine fund raising and during Campaign fund raising, the central development office should have primary responsibility for the annual fund, the maintenance of the alumni database, and the maintenance of gift records. In addition, during Campaign fund raising only, the majority of respondents also gave the central development office primary responsibility for major individual gifts and major foundation gifts. Almost as many believed that, during a Capital Campaign, the central office should have primary responsibility for major corporate gifts. The consensus on the assignment of primary responsibility for major individual, corporate, and foundation gifts during a Campaign showed a firm belief in a strong central development office (see figure 5). Few of those who withheld primary responsibility for major gift efforts from the central office assigned it to the academic unit office. Instead they claimed that it should be evenly held. However, during

Figure 5. Responsibilities of the Central Office
(aggregate group agreement)

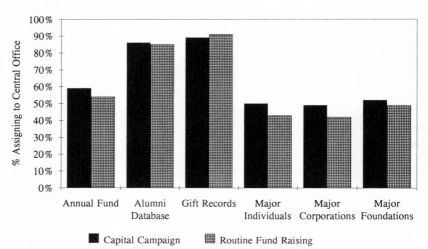

routine, non-Campaign fund raising, the majority shifted away from giving the responsibility to the central development office and assigned it to the academic units or to be evenly held.

A majority of all the development officers indicated that the responsibility for identifying prospective donors should be evenly held between the academic units and the central office both during routine fund raising and during a Campaign. Almost as many believed that the responsibility for setting fund-raising priorities and stewardship of gifts should be evenly held between the academic units and the central office during both routine and Campaign fund raising (see figure 6).

In the aggregate group of responses, CUDOs outnumbered AUDOs. Thirty-five percent of those surveyed were AUDOs and 65 percent were CUDOs. The responses were proportional to the requests: 36 percent of the responses came from AUDOs and 64 percent came from CUDOs (see figure 7). Thus, the respondent group has many more CUDOs than AUDOs. The assignment by this aggregate group of most fund-raising responsibilities to the central development office may, in fact, be influenced by the disproportionate representation of the central development officer in the group. Further analysis showed that on many issues,

Figure 6. Responsibilities to be Evenly Held (aggregate group agreement)

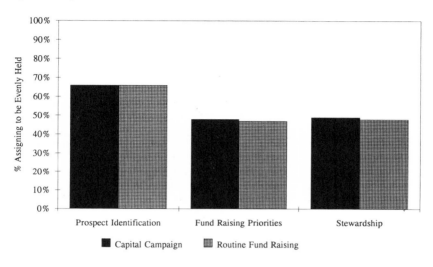

Figure 7. Survey Respondents by Group

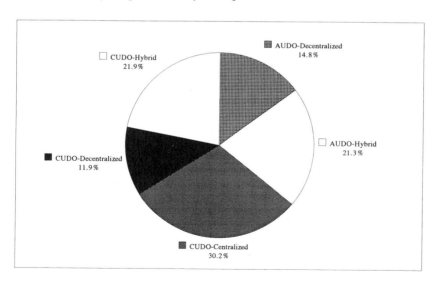

Figure 8. Responsibility for the Alumni Database (in routine fund raising)

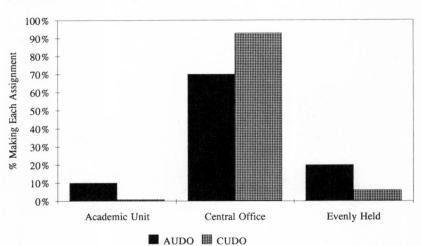

CUDOs and AUDOs responded differently about the assignment of responsibility. Therefore, the fact that the aggregate group is dominated by CUDOs masks some helpful and important currents of opinion among development professionals.

Comparison Group Responses: Areas of Agreement

The aggregate group of respondents includes the following subgroups: (1) CUDOs in fully centralized systems, (2) CUDOs in fully decentralized systems, (3) CUDOs in hybrid systems, (4) AUDOs in fully decentralized systems, (5) AUDOs in hybrid systems.

When the responses are segmented into these groups, some of the patterns of agreement among development officers are strongly confirmed. Regardless of whether a development officer is an AUDO or a CUDO, and regardless of whether the development officer works in a fully centralized, fully decentralized, or hybrid system, the majority of each group stated that the central office should maintain the alumni databases and the gift records. Over 90 percent of CUDOs said the primary responsibility for the alumni databases should always be in

Figure 9. Responsibility for Gift Records (in routine fund raising)

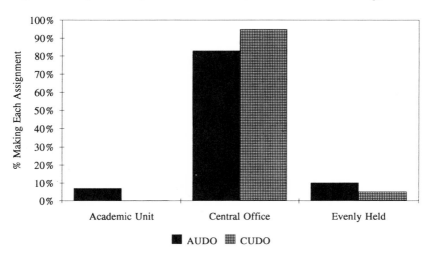

the central office. Seventy percent of AUDOs would assign it there, with most of the rest saying that it should be evenly held (see figure 8).

Regardless of the comparison group, most development officers also agreed that the central office should bear the responsibility for maintaining gift records. None of the CUDOs would assign this responsibility to the academic units and less than 10 percent of them said it should be evenly held. Ten percent or less of the AUDOs would assign this responsibility to the academic unit offices or have it be evenly held during routine fund-raising efforts. During a Campaign, a few more AUDOs assigned it to the academic unit or assigned it to be evenly held (see figure 9).

More than 50 percent of the members of each group would assign the responsibility for prospect identification to be evenly held by the central and academic unit offices both when a Campaign is in progress and when it is not (see figure 10).

These data indicated that the chief university development officer should have strong support in establishing an efficient and effective development services program within the central office. Few would resist the allocation to the central development office of resources to implement a database management and recordkeeping system,

Figure 10. Responsibility for Identifying Prospects
(in routine fund raising)

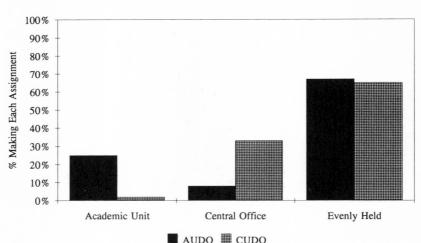

which serves all development officers and supports all development
activities.

Comparison Group Responses: Areas of Disagreement

Analysis of the responses within groups also showed considerable
disagreement. The data indicated that the division of responsibility
often is assessed differently by CUDOs and AUDOs. At times the division was also different among CUDOs in the various management
systems and different between AUDOs in fully decentralized and those
in hybrid systems. Disagreement was significant in the following areas.

Annual Fund

Although an absolute majority of development officers would assign responsibility for annual fund to the central office, when the
responses were analyzed by group, the agreement disappeared. While
CUDOs more often said that the responsibility should be with the central office, AUDOs leaned slightly toward the academic unit, but disagreement is more common than agreement on this issue (see figure 11).

Figure 11. Responsibility for the Annual Fund (in routine fund raising)

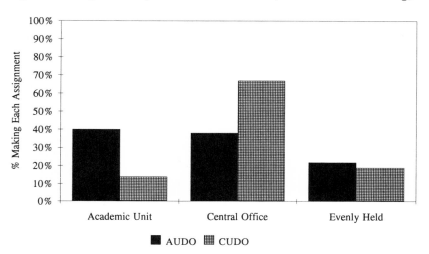

The interviews with deans and development officers cast some light on the annual fund issue. The disagreement over responsibility for the annual fund program was apparent in the interviews as well as in the survey responses, but the disagreement did not concern the design, implementation, or supervision of annual fund. All comments indicated that the central development office was best equipped to run the annual fund program with professional skill and economies of scale.

The dissention concerned the designation of money raised from the annual fund appeal. Assuming that the respondents to the final survey were influenced by the same concerns as those in the case studies, development officers probably assigned responsibility for annual fund to the central office at institutions where all annual fund receipts were clearly earmarked for the unrestricted fund, as well as at institutions where donors were given clear control over the designation of their gifts. In cases where donors were encouraged to give to the unrestricted fund but designation to another fund was accepted when the donor insisted, responsibility was more likely to be assigned by academic unit development officers to the academic unit. In the case studies, academic unit leaders were willing to take responsibility for running the annual fund if they believed that it could substantially increase the amount of money designated for their units.

Figure 12. Responsibility for Major Gifts (in routine fund raising)

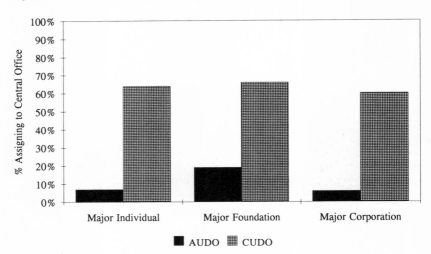

Major Individual Gifts

Although the aggregate analysis showed consensus that the central office, during a Campaign, should have primary responsibility for major individual gifts, significant disagreement was evident between CUDOs and AUDOs. During routine fund raising, a majority of CUDOs placed the responsibility with the central office while a majority of AUDOs placed it with the academic unit. When the institution is in a Capital Campaign, even more of the CUDOs placed the responsibility with the central office. The AUDOs, if they moved the responsibility at all, moved it to being evenly held (figure 12).

During one interview, a dean at Hybrid University talked about his long-term cultivation of major donors. He said that for years he had been visiting with and involving major donors in his planning and brainstorming about the college's objectives. He also had been dropping hints about the college's needs and priorities. As a result, the donors have close ties to the college and feel a sense of involvement—even ownership—for implementation of the college's action plan. He and others at the college have been paying attention to the donors and treating them well. When the AUDO or a development officer from the central staff asks them to make a gift, the donors tend to

Figure 13. Responsibility for Setting Fund-raising Priorities (in routine fund raising)

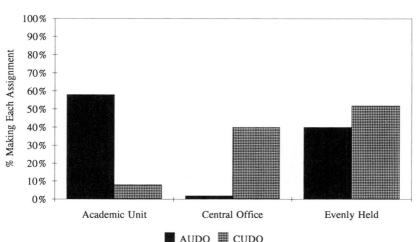

indicate their specific interest in this school. The AUDO then prepares a proposal. The school gets the gift. The dean says, "It's because we have been doing our job and giving priority attention to fund raising and external relations all along."

Major Corporate Gifts

The pattern of disagreement evident when assigning responsibility for major corporate gifts paralleled the one for major individual gifts. CUDOs most often assigned the responsibility to the central office. AUDOs assigned it to the academic unit offices. When the institution is in a Capital Campaign, AUDOs shifted the responsibility toward being evenly held (see figure 13).

Major Foundation Gifts

As with other major donor prospects, AUDOs and CUDOs disagreed on who should have primary responsibility for major foundation gifts. Slightly more than one quarter of CUDOs and slightly more than one third of AUDOs assigned the responsibility to be evenly held when the institution is not in a Capital Campaign. The same percentage of

Figure 14. Responsibility for Stewardship (in routine fund raising)

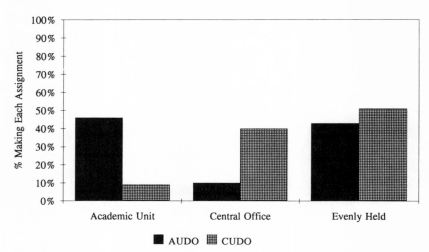

CUDOs but almost one half of AUDOs assigned it evenly during a Capital Campaign. Less than 10 percent of CUDOs assigned this responsibility to the academic units in either situation. Over 40 percent of AUDOs thought the responsibility should be with the academic units when not in a Campaign while almost 30 percent assigned the responsibility to the academic units when in a Campaign (figure 12).

Setting Development Priorities

Although the aggregate results indicated that there was consensus that responsibility for setting development priorities should be evenly held, the group analyses show a different pattern. Over half of the CUDOs would have the primary responsibility for setting development priorities be evenly held when an institution is not in a Campaign, while only 8 percent of them would have the academic units take the responsibility. Of the AUDOs, 58 percent would have the academic units be primarily responsible when not in a Campaign, with another 40 percent having it be evenly held. During a Campaign, while all groups would shift slightly toward giving the central office primary responsibility, most development officers would maintain it evenly held (see figure 13).

Stewardship of Gifts

Although most of the aggregate group indicated that stewardship should be an evenly held responsibility, the disagreement between AUDOs and CUDOs shows strongly in the group analyses. While only 9 percent of CUDOs believed that the academic unit should have primary responsibility for stewardship of gifts during routine fund raising and only 8 percent during a Campaign, 46 percent of AUDOs believed that the academic unit should have this responsibility when not in a Campaign and 34 percent when in a campaign. Over 40 percent of both CUDOs and AUDOs said the responsibility should be evenly held in both cases (see figure 14).

Stewardship of large gifts is both a development and an administrative responsibility. The university and the major donor should come to an agreement (which should always be specified in writing) on the use of a specific contribution. Administrative policies should be implemented to assure that the terms of the agreement are met. Assuring that the donor has the pleasure of seeing the results of his or her philanthropic action will, from a development point of view, help prepare the donor to make additional gifts. The disagreement over who should be responsible for stewardship is often complicated by confusion between the administrative and development functions of stewardship.

Comparison Group Responses: Areas with No Dominant Pattern

Preparation of a Case Statement

A dean needs a case statement to demonstrate the clarity of the plan for enhancing the academic unit. There is no format for this case statement. It can be an inspiring essay prepared on a word processor, it can be a glossy publication, or it can be a video presentation. It can be inexpensive or costly, informal or formal, traditional or innovative. The primary requirement is that it have academic substance.

Over 40 percent of CUDOs in fully centralized institutions believed that the responsibility for preparing the case statement should be evenly held both during a Campaign and when not in a Campaign. It was not surprising that in a centralized system, the responsibility for

Figure 15. Responsibility for the Case Statement
(in routine fund raising)

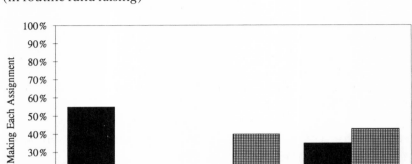

production of the case statement would stay with the central office or be evenly held. If the responsibility were with the academic unit, there would be no one whose job it was primarily to design and produce the case statement. But the thinking reflected in the case statement has to come from the person with the academic plan.

CUDOs in decentralized systems would give primary responsibility to the academic unit office slightly more often than would CUDOs in centralized systems, but only when the institution was not in a Campaign.

Just over 50 percent of AUDOs would give primary responsibility for the preparation of the case statement to the academic unit office when not in a Campaign, with most of the rest saying it should be evenly held. During a Campaign, about half of those AUDOs would shift the responsibility toward the central office or toward being evenly held (see figure 15.)

Preparation of a Proposal

AUDOs most often would place responsibility for preparing proposals in the academic units while CUDOs most often would have it evenly held (see figure 16).

Figure 16. Responsibility for Proposal Preparation
(in routine fund raising)

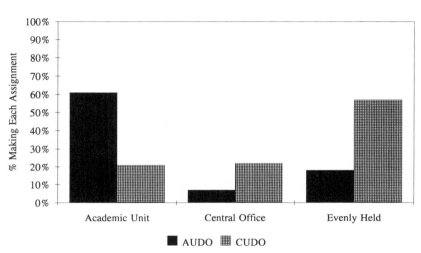

One of the deans at Central University told me that he sometimes had the impression that raising money was the goal of a centralized office. He said that the goal of the academic unit was "raising money to do something with." In his opinion, the latter goal lead to both the establishment of more specific and attainable objectives and the presentation of more convincing proposals. It would therefore bring more support, he believed.

This same dean was convinced that centralization of proposal preparation made more work for the faculty and was less effective with potential donors. Because the central development officers were unfamiliar with the real expertise and the real needs of the school, they often built the conceptual framework for a proposed project based only on the perceived or stated interests of a prospective donor. The central office would then ask the academic unit to "flesh out" the proposal. The dean believed that this process was the reverse of the proper one. He thought that the academic unit should design and write the proposal; the central office should add the bells, whistles, and boilerplate.

Summary

As would be expected given the fact that CUDOs outnumber AUDOs in the aggregate group of all development officers, given the relative youth of decentralization, and given the fact that development must play a leadership role in the highest levels of university management, a majority of the aggregate group favored assigning the responsibility for most tasks to the central development office or to be evenly held by the central office and the dean's offices.

Regardless of whether they were AUDOs or CUDOs, the majority of development officers believed that alumni records and gift data should be maintained centrally and that the responsibility for prospect research should be shared evenly. However, CUDOs and AUDOs disagreed strongly on the assignment of other responsibilities, particularly on those related to the management of the relationship between the potential donor and the University. AUDOs usually believed that AUDOs should manage the interaction with donors; CUDOs believed that CUDOs should.

8 | *Coordination and Control*

Having sorted out the factors that can influence AUDO success and having negotiated an effective division of responsibilities for development tasks, a dean can turn to some other challenging managerial issues, including coordination and control.

During the interviews, everyone voiced concern about coordination of development activities to avoid multiple or inappropriate solicitations. To follow up on these concerns, I sought data on the effectiveness of systems used to track cultivation, solicitation, and stewardship activities.

At Central University and Hybrid University, both central academic and central development leaders said that coordination was the single most important issue that the structure of the development office had to manage. Some management literature supports the view that coordination and control are essential in maintaining unified movement within centralized management models (Martin and Moore, 1985, pp. 57–63). But the deans did not rank the importance of coordination quite so high. At Hybrid University, one dean said that he saw coordination and control as management problems, not structural problems. He said that coordination and control are always necessary, but since some universities with decentralized systems have great fund-raising success, it is obvious that a university doesn't have to centralize to assure appropriate coordination and control.

At Decentral University, most of those interviewed thought that the coordination and control issue was exaggerated. Nevertheless, they agreed that coordination was important. The president said he was satisfied that the decentralized system was best for his institution. However, he was not yet satisfied with the level of coordination. He wanted a protocol that provided better lines of communication to keep him informed of who was talking to whom and who was likely to be more successful in getting support from a specific individual or organization.

The president insisted that he wanted to avoid turning prospect management and information-sharing into control of all gifts, and that he definitely was not concerned about maintaining control over gift designation. He said that his job was to plan for the future and to oversee the implementation of the mission. He believed that the mission should be an umbrella, uniting and protecting a number of flexible products that varied according to the innovation and ingenuity of the people in the academic units. The educational output could have one shape this year and another next year, while still moving in an appropriate direction. The faculty in the units should move the institution into the areas where they have the greatest expertise. Senior administrators cannot know faculty expertise better than the faculty itself does. Units cannot be "totally unfettered," but he claimed to not like the idea of "control." Management literature supports his comments. In decentralized systems, control is less important, while coordination is often horizontal as well as vertical (Martin and Moore, 1985, p. 60).

The AUDOs at Decentral University stressed the importance and effectiveness of horizontal coordination. They regularly talked to each other about prospects and arranged their cultivation activities to supplement and complement each other's. They thought that discussion of competition among the academic units over prospects is blown out of proportion. In their experience, academic units were seldom ready to approach a major donor simultaneously. If the potential donor is properly involved in the programs and plans of more than one component of the university, both will be able to discuss gifts with the donor. Assuming that the prospective donor has been working with the various components of the university and is interested in the implementation of more than one academic plan, more than one proposal can be submitted. Even large companies seldom object to receiving excellent, reasonable, and well conceived proposals for a number of projects that are clearly within the company's areas of interest. The issues are appropriate cultivation of donor interest, timing, and quality assurance.

Even if you accept this unorthodox view, coordination of the prospect pool is necessary to avoid inappropriate multiple solicitations of donors. These development officers and their vice president said that the deans should be responsible for coordinating contacts with the most sensitive major prospects through their academic deans' council. Other prospects should be assigned through a peer review system, which uses the respect for and confidence in each other that the academic unit development officers have, rather than relying on a central development officer. In a decentralized system, the Director of Corporate and Foundation Relations may have less experience and stature than the AUDOs. Peer review is, therefore, more effective.

The vice president of Decentral University believed that a research university needs "a cohesive systematic development program and a good prospect management system, where people are not running around willy-nilly calling on everybody, and where there is a carefully planned strategy for raising money with development officers reporting back to a central office." But his president, deans, and AUDOs were convinced that these goals were attainable without increasing centralization.

One of the Decentral University deans said that the disadvantages to their coordination and control system were based on poor management at the central development office level. The central development office's attempts at coordination vacillated between being inadequate and being overly constraining. Either no one was helping the deans avoid bumping into one another in the outer office of a potential major donor or the deans and their development officers were spending too many hours filling out reports on who they were visiting, without getting any feedback on their activities, on those of the other deans, or on those undertaken directly by the central office.

The vice president of Decentral University said that a campus-wide dissatisfaction with the coordination of development activities arose because each school began its fund raising independently and with some annoyance that the central office did not provide the service it desired. Now, even with all new central office staff, some resistance persisted to building a cooperative attitude. The vice president believed the resistance to cooperation was built into the system. When development officers met to discuss prospects and priorities, they came to a consensus on most topics. Agreement was occasionally not complete on one prospect or proposal. Since the development officers were not accountable to the chair of the coordination council, who was a central development officer, but only to their deans, the basic disagreement persisted. The development officers who disagreed would continue to believe that they should do the best thing for their individual colleges until, at some point, conflict would occur. To date, according to the vice president, no procedure existed for settling such conflicts, or for derailing the problems before they became conflicts.

Centralized coordination and control do not necessarily operate smoothly either. The acting president of the Central University emphasized that coordination and control of the prospect pool was essential to effective fund raising and that centralization was the best way to assure this goal. His deans were supposed to work through the central development office, which, he said, "causes a slight degree of friction or maybe a larger than slight degree of friction when they don't." During the recent Capital Campaign, fund-raising initiatives "had to be tightly tied together because we were approaching so many companies and individuals." One dean had established a relationship with several companies ten or fifteen years before for scholarship aid. Corporate enthusiasm for this type of support had diminished recently. The university needed to go to those firms in the Campaign and wanted to present many opportunities for gifts, not all in the school where the original ties had existed. The central development office was able to make professional judgments about which companies would be most receptive to which requests, using previously established relationships between the university and the company as sources of information rather than as limiting factors.

A centralized development operation, according to the vice president, provides the institution with a single list of all prospective donors and a unified strategy for dealing with each of them. The development office staff, under the leadership of a senior development professional, can evaluate those prospects and match their interests with activities in the various colleges of the university. The central office starts with the prospects and their interests rather than starting with the colleges and their interests. The deans provide lists of their colleges' needs and these lists are the source of information about college interests. The central staff tries to make good links between the colleges and the donors. The vice president believes that the central staff is adequate to help each of the colleges provide appropriate attention to each potential donor.

The potential animosity, which the acting president mentioned that such control might engender, displayed itself vividly in a comment from one of the deans: "As you may have guessed, I'm not totally enthusiastic about this centralized system. In fact, quite the opposite. We've been told for years that little boys should mind their manners and march on with the team and everything would come out well in the end. Well, it hasn't." The deans said they believed that convincing case statements that are based on strong academic plans attract support, not coordination and control.

As at Central University, at Hybrid University I heard that centralized management of the development office is necessary in order to maintain adequate coordination and control of the prospect pool. Particularly when the institution is preparing for or conducting a Capital Campaign, the university must have a central source of information and of decision making concerning all approaches to prospective and current donors. Many believed that the management system that the University has created takes advantage of most of the good aspects of decentralization without foregoing this essential advantage of centralization.

Hybrid University AUDOs praised their system for prospect management and tracking of solicitations. It decreased the occurrence of multiple solicitations to individuals and organizational funding sources. It encouraged open discussion of prospects and their interests. It assured that no prospect was assigned without a public discussion and there was no secrecy about prospective donors.

A former employee of Hybrid University also participated in the case study. In his opinion, the tracking system used by the university was too dependent on technology. He believed that since development will always be a "high touch" business, electronic tracking will always be inadequate. A tracking system must be flexible. It must not penalize a development officer for admitting that the college does not yet have a relationship with a potential donor but intends to establish one. It must allow for the fact that while some organizations and individuals favor multiple solicitations, others do not. It must also allow for the entry of newcomers into the tracking system. The

Figure 17. Tracking Development Activities

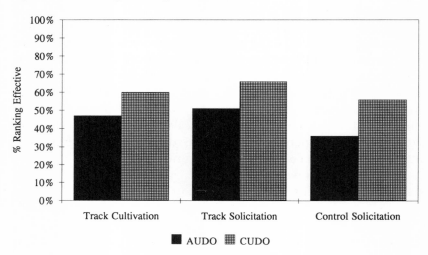

priority given to established relationships must be tempered in order to allow newcomers to build relationships.

Like the AUDOs at Decentral University, those at Hybrid University pointed out that coordination and control may not be as critical as others claim it to be. They said that since Hybrid University is large and complex, it has many excellent programs. They find that more than one of these programs can be of interest to the same potential donor.

One of the Hybrid University deans told me that he believed that as the university's development program matured and donors became more involved in the areas of the university where they had interest, the donors would become more willing to entertain multiple pro-posals. In addition, as the university's development program matured it would build a broader pool of prospective donors and a stronger volunteer structure so that the same people were not being asked time and again for gifts and assistance. The dean believed that at that point the need for a centralized development operation would diminish and the disadvantages of even their modified level of centralization would outweigh the advantages.

Most of the institutions represented in the case studies and the survey had university-wide systems for tracking the cultivation of donors (80 percent), for tracking the solicitation of gifts (87 percent), and for preventing inappropriate multiple solicitations of donors (82 percent). The systems were perceived as being only moderately effective (see figure 17). On a continuum from ineffective to effective, 55 percent of the respondents considered their institution's systems for tracking the cultivation of donors to be closer to effective than to ineffective. Sixty-one percent of them considered the tracking of solicitation of donors to be closer to effective than to ineffective, and 56 percent of them considered the system for preventing inappropriate multiple solicitations to be closer to effective. More CUDOs than AUDOs rated the systems effective.

9 | *Autonomy and the Balance of Power*

WHEREAS IN THE PREVIOUS CHAPTER the discussion focused on control of the fund-raising activities of deans and development officers, this chapter is concerned with who controls the university itself. Decentralization of development affects the university's autonomy on two levels—it can change the balance of power on campus and it can affect the university's ability to set its own priorities.

The rationale for centralizing fund raising is based on the need for control of the university's fund-raising program, particularly control of the contacts with potential donors. On the contrary, the rationale for decentralizing fund raising is based on the need for deans to take the initiative in the development process of their colleges. When decentralization occurs, the deans increase their contacts with the affluent and influential members of the university's constituency. They raise money outside of the university resource allocation process. They cultivate friendships with people whose money and power can affect the university's internal processes.

The president of Decentral University told me that he was convinced that deans who succeeded in fund-raising activities gained power among their fellow deans. Decentralization of development activities created a danger of sending a "cleaver into carefully crafted teamwork." Those who raised more money could spend more and were envied. Those who built strong groups of advocates to help them raise money could rely on those advocates to lobby with the university and state officials in favor of the college.

He said that fund-raising success also gave deans "a sense that they have one more tool in the arsenal" when negotiating with the president. It contributed to a sense of "independence." The president said that some might think that allowing deans to have development officers gave them *too* much power, but he believed that the benefit of having the deans be fully committed to and involved in the fund-raising efforts of the university outweighed the disadvantages of changing the power balance in the institution. A little discomfort can be good for an organization, he thought.

Decentralization of development introduces additional factors into the power equation. Power is based on (1) control of a resource, a technical skill, or an important body of knowledge; (2) legal prerogatives; or (3) access to people who can provide (1) or (2) (Mintzberg, 1983, p. 24). A professional development officer brings to the academic unit technical skills and a body of knowledge much needed by, and in great demand at, the university. Institutional leaders are eager to learn how to increase their resources, how to convince major individual and organizational donors to invest their philanthropic dollars in the programs of the university, and how to attract alumni support. Successful development programs employ known and tested processes that the development officer is skilled in implementing. The development officer helps the academic unit to increase its resources.

Many of those interviewed said that an academic unit with an effective development officer gained power within the institution. The academic unit development officers at Hybrid University said they believed that a successful development operation increased the power and, to an extent, the prestige of a dean at their university.

Having academic unit development offices may promote at least the perception of increased independence from the rest of the university. An effective academic unit development program will bring into the unit some private dollars that the dean can spend outside of the university's normal budget constraints. The development office will also build a group of influential volunteers to be advocates for the unit and help with fund-raising strategy and implementation. The information gathered to prepare credible proposals can also indirectly help the unit receive a larger share of internal resources.

The Decentral University deans told me that having an effective development operation increased their interaction with influential members of the business community and provided them with an additional staff member who was particularly skilled at gathering information.

Blau's (1964) theories of social exchange contribute to this discussion. An organization that receives a larger amount of philanthropic support than its peers is in a position to be able to contribute disproportionately more to its constituents—more research, better prepared alumni, increased community service. Within an institution that has decentralized its development operation, a parallel phenomenon occurs. As the subunit receives more philanthropic support, it is able to contribute more to the university as a whole. Other subunits, which have only base university support or have less philanthropic support to add to their base support, cannot contribute as much. The richer subunit becomes more powerful as it contributes more prestige, more successful alumni, more publications, more service to the university and the community that the university serves. It can then command a larger share of the base support as well. The enhanced ability of a richer academic unit to contribute to the measurable achievements of the university will command increased support for the unit over competing institutional components.

The president of the institution may have mixed feelings about a management system that grants deans the mechanism for enhancing their power. If development is centrally controlled, this resource belongs to the president.

The power relationships between the university and its donors are an ongoing concern regardless of the degree of centralization of the development operation (Curti and Nash, 1965, pp. 213–14; Hofstadter and Metzger, 1955, pp. 140–45; Rudolph, 1962, pp. 352–53; Veysey, 1965, pp. 346–50). This power relationship is particularly important because it affects the university's ability to set its own priorities. Institutions seek donors whose interests overlap with the goals of the college or university. Institutional leaders try to avoid accepting gifts that skew priorities, drain resources from core programs, or give the donor an opportunity to dictate internal policy such as personnel decisions or admission decisions. Since the ends sought by the donor and recipient are seldom identical, a creative tension develops that keeps each responsive to the other and helps to expand the perspective of each (McDonald, 1950, pp. 63–69).

The ability of a university to set its own priorities might theoretically be affected by a donor whose gift carries contingent conditions. This issue is discussed by many authors including Curti and Nash

(1965), Hofstadter and Metzger (1955), Rudolph (1962), and Veysey (1965). Those interviewed during the case studies believed that this was not a significant problem as long as university priorities were clearly set. They were convinced that the academic and development leaders working with the potential donor would and could either influence the donor to designate the gift for a priority program or have the institution walk away from the gift.

The power of gifts to change university priorities has now been carefully and extensively described (Kelly, 1991, pp. 211–34). A dean needs to be aware of that power and alert to both its positive and negative effects. A dean, better than a central development officer, can assure that a gift fits with the expertise and priority of the individual college. A dean at Hybrid University told me that he knew he could "look the donor in the eye (they've been rejected before) and say I don't want to accept that gift exactly as described because the area has a bad image in our field. But I think we can do something which will fit your goals even better by . . ." The dean believed he was less likely than a CUDO to antagonize the potential donor with such a message because his job is to focus on academic issues, not resource issues.

When a dean has worked with a donor over the years and developed a good relationship, he or she is better able to describe to the donor the needs and strengths of the college. He or she can work with a donor to design a program that fits both of their visions of a better college.

Major gifts have a real impact on the future of individual colleges and, through the colleges, on the university as a whole. To assure that a gift does not change the priorities of the institution, the recipient has to be able to communicate well with the donor about those priorities. In a university with decentralized academic management, it is the dean who can best address the question of priorities. Thus, the dean is in the best position for dealing directly with the donor. However, the president is the ultimate spokesperson for the university, assuring the donor that the gift meets an institutional priority and is important to the whole institution. But presidents and their staffs are not, at least according to the deans I interviewed, the best negotiators of the purpose of the gift. They cannot have as deep an understanding of the need being addressed by the gift and the impact that the gift will make on the institution.

Private gifts can and do alter institutional priorities. At institutions represented by 47 percent of the respondents to my survey, a major gift had, in the past, caused a significant shift in the academic priorities of an academic unit. The solicitation of the gift was managed jointly by the academic unit and the central office in the majority of the cases: 67 percent said jointly, 7 percent said central, and 26 percent said academic unit. In most cases the shift in priorities was readily accepted by both the academic unit and the central administration: "by the academic unit," 94 percent said yes; "by the central administration," 95 percent said yes.

There were over 80 percent of CUDOs in fully centralized systems, over 70 percent of CUDOs in fully decentralized systems, but only 47 percent of CUDOs in hybrid systems who indicated that a major gift had at some time caused a shift in the academic priorities. Fewer AUDOs noted such a shift: 52 percent of them in fully decentralized systems and 37 percent in hybrid systems. Both AUDOs and CUDOs at hybrid universities noted fewer priorities changes based on gifts.

My interviews highlighted a concern that a central development officer and an academic unit development officer might have different views on institutional priorities. One dean gave the example of a gift accepted for his unit by the central office. The gift was designated for a program that was not a current priority and was draining resources from more important programs. He said that the gift "is something we need and someday will really need badly, so it isn't a total loss. But we weren't ready and it is driving other expenditures, which is causing severe dislocations in our operating in the meantime. The expenditures are far in excess of the gift". The dean believed that if the development officer were working for the school directly, not only would gifts be accepted only when they would really help the school, but it would also be easier to track expenditures from gift monies and therefore provide better stewardship.

In contrast, a story by the vice president of Decentral University gave an example of a major gift accepted by an academic unit for a program that was low on the university's priority list. An AUDO identified and made contact with a potential donor who previously had little contact with the university. The donor made a gift, several years later, after considerably more contact with both college- and university-level academic and development leaders. The donor designated a

Figure 18. The Effect of Decentralization on the Dean's Power

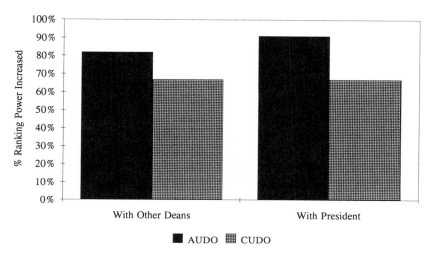

large part of the gift for a program at the AUDO's college, even though enhancement of that program was not a university priority.

No one indicated that the two gifts mentioned above should have been rejected by their institutions but that the situations were less than ideal. The examples made it clear that private gifts can and do alter institutional priorities.

The survey also pursued these power and autonomy issues (see figure 18). A high level of private support for an academic unit increased the dean's power among other deans according to 73 percent of the respondents. The level of private support increased the dean's power with the president according to 75 percent of respondents. All groups of respondents agreed. CUDOs in fully centralized systems were the least likely to see a relationship between a dean's power and the amount of private support for that dean's academic unit.

10 | *The Management of Volunteers*

VOLUNTEERS ARE A KEY to successful fund raising. A volunteer is a person who is not paid by the university, yet who provides time and service to help the university. Trustees, members of advisory boards, outside experts who accept faculty invitations to lecture to classes, alumni association officers, are all volunteers.

Many volunteers bring personal wealth, wisdom, experience, and power to their university service. They bring access to affluence and influence. An effective development operation will necessarily be grounded in the interest and involvement of volunteers. The development officer will help the academic unit identify alumni, community, and business leaders who will be strong and articulate advocates. When these leaders become donors themselves they will directly influence others to support the programs in which they have invested.

Having an AUDO facilitates effective use of volunteers. Each of the deans at Decentral University had a board of volunteer advisors for his school. Neither board was initially established primarily as a development board; in fact, both boards were established before the dean had hired a development officer. The boards advised the dean on a variety of academic and external relations issues. Each board had become more involved in development activities as the board matured. Board members became knowledgeable about the school's needs and priorities through board service. They helped to interest potential donors who were not board members in the activities of the school. The boards worked closely with the dean and his development officer. Some of the members of these boards also served on the university-wide development board, bringing their knowledge of the school's needs to the discussions of university-wide development activities.

Without an AUDO, the dean is unlikely to have the necessary staff support to use volunteers effectively. Neither academic unit at Central University had a volunteer board that was active in cultivation or solicitation of prospective donors. The deans stated that if they had a decentralized system, they would have more incentive to build an effective volunteer structure. One of the deans said that he thought a major disadvantage to centralization was that it gave him an excuse to do nothing but complain about fund raising. He said he was not even actively communicating with alumni through events or a newsletter. He thought perhaps it wasn't allowed.

A dean at Hybrid University said he had an alumni board but not a development advisory board. He wanted to establish a development board but it was not approved because the central development office did not want "ten mini-campaigns going on during the central campaign." The alumni board helped with external relations but not directly with fund raising.

A dean should seek a development officer who can work directly with high-level volunteers. A less senior officer cannot represent the dean adequately with volunteers in top-level positions with outside organizations. Nor is a dean likely to be comfortable giving a novice full access to the college's most important friends. While a volunteer board enhances the academic unit's opportunity for success in philanthropic endeavors, the dean needs senior level staff support for that board.

11 | *The Flow of Communication*

INFORMATION is one of a university's primary resources. People who have information have power. A dean's power is sometimes judged by how often he or she knows important things before most others know them. Access to information can be valued as highly as access to money.

A dean who is responsible for fund raising needs to obtain information about trends, initiatives, and interests in the philanthropic community and about development activities across the campus. The dean also needs to share specific information about academic unit development activities and central development office development activities with the CUDO and the president, and needs to know what other deans are doing to identify, cultivate, and solicit contributions. It is also important that the president be kept informed about and involved in the dean's development activities.

Sharing information is serious business. Everyone I interviewed during this study talked about communication. After saying that he did not want to control the contacts between the deans and prospective donors, the president of Decentral University went on to say that he needed a better mechanism for knowing what cultivation, solicitation, and stewardship activities were occurring. He dreaded the possibility that he would meet a university donor or prospective donor and be unaware of a recent contact. He wanted to have a view of the big picture. He wanted to understand and influence the interaction with donors, but not to direct or produce every strategy.

Information flow can be a complex issue for the development officers of a large university. The central office needs to be kept informed of new initiatives and interests at the schools. The academic units need to be kept informed of contacts between the central office and

Figure 19. Development Officers as a Source of Internal Information

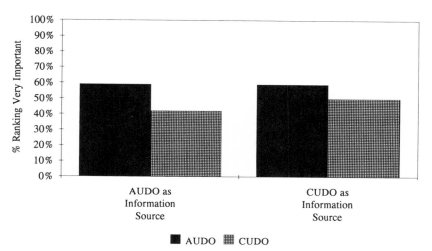

potential donors. When there are departments within the schools that are very active on a development project, the dean of the school must be in the information loop.

A development officer can be a particularly helpful source of information for a dean about university-wide development activities (see figure 19). A Decentral University dean told me that his AUDO was invaluable in providing information. She regularly talked to key alumni about their companies, their impressions of the college and its graduates, their ideas for the future of engineering in the region. Similarly, she met regularly, both formally and informally, with her peers from the other colleges on campus. This senior development officer network was very effective for keeping in touch with the other colleges' news and concerns. If this dean ever had to give up having his own development officer, he would particularly miss the information she gathered in the normal course of doing her job. Even if her office had to be located outside of the academic unit, he would lose some of the communication advantage that she brought to him. By working regularly with faculty and with other development officers, she brought him more current information about the mood and activity of the campus than he could ever hope to gather through formal channels.

Figure 20. Development Officers as a Source of External Information

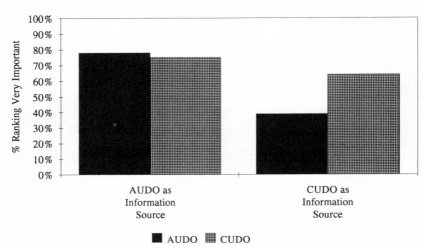

He believed that because of her efforts, his responses to faculty and community issues were enhanced.

Surveyed development officers tended to say that AUDOs also played an important role in keeping the dean and the college informed about external events and trends. On the survey, more than half of CUDOs said the AUDO played a very important role and almost 75 percent of AUDOs said the same. Development officers indicated that the central development office, although not quite as strongly as the academic unit development office, also helped keep the deans and colleges informed (see figure 20).

Both academic and development leaders at all the universities talked about the need for clear and candid communication. Many deans and development officers criticized the processes at their institutions for sharing information about development activities. There were harsh critics both at the academic unit level and at the university level. There were individuals at both levels who were complimentary of their institution's communication processes. Although many authors discuss the importance of communication in organizations (see Argyris, 1964; Etzioni, 1964; Likert, 1967; Odiorne, 1965), few compare communication in centralized and decentralized organiza-

Figure 21. Assessment of Upward and Downward Communication within the System

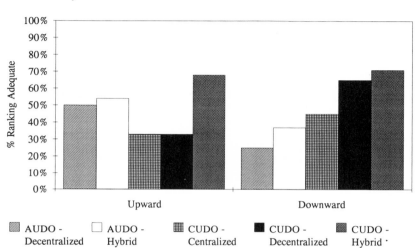

tions. Drucker (1954) claims that decentralization improves the timeliness and effectiveness of communication.

The survey participants rated communication about development activities upward from the academic units to the central development office and downward from the central development office to the academic units. In each case they stated whether it was adequate, neutral, or inadequate. By a two-to-one margin, AUDOs said upward communication was adequate. The CUDOs in hybrid systems agreed; 68 percent of them rated communication about development upward from the academic units to the central office adequate. Only about one-third of the CUDOs at decentralized or centralized universities rated it adequate. (See figure 21.)

The vice president at Hybrid University fit the pattern of the survey results, saying that all AUDOs met weekly with the central development office staff to discuss prospect-related activities and plans. As a result, he was confident that he could provide accurate and timely information to the president.

However, although only 22 percent of AUDOs said upward communication was inadequate, 46 percent of them said that downward communication provided about the central office's development activities and those of other colleges was inadequate. At Hybrid University, even with weekly meetings between AUDOs and the central staff, the AUDOs did not feel that they were being provided with adequate information about the central development officers' donor-related activities.

The CUDOs in hybrid and decentralized systems indicated that they believed downward communication was adequate (71 percent and 65 percent). But the interviews indicated that communication from the central development office to the academic units at Central University was inadequate and a cause of much of the dissatisfaction the deans expressed toward the development program of the university. The CUDOs in centralized systems apparently recognized a similar problem since fewer than half of them rated downward communication from themselves to academic units as adequate.

The importance of open communication was apparent in the comments of a Central University dean. He said that their recent Campaign is a credit to the central development office and that most universities would envy such success. The central office clearly knows what it's doing. "I guess I would be a lot happier with it if it were more open centralization or if it were reaching out to understand who we are, what we do, how to represent us, and then say, ok, but we'll coordinate centrally." When the Campaign began, the deans were asked to state their schools' needs for the central development staff. Admitting to cynicism, the dean said he believes that when all the needs were reviewed, only the most flashy were given serious consideration. The problem, in his opinion, is that to a large degree, centralized means secret. The deans never know the basis for the central office's decisions. "It's centralized and secret, and that's what troubles me."

12 | *The Development Officer and the Faculty*

THE RELATIONSHIP between the development officers and the faculty at many institutions was summed up by one of the deans at Central University. He told me that development officers think that all faculty members are so parochial that you can't let them talk to donors and, conversely, that faculty members think that all development officers are so sleazy that you can't let them talk to your corporate contacts.

A dean with responsibility for fund raising has a serious task in trying to break down the stereotypical barriers between development officers and faculty so that the advancement goals of the college can be met. Too often they have such different points of view that they do not communicate well with one another. In more than a few cases, as the Central University dean pointed out, there is no mutual respect for their points of view.

My survey asked development officers whether they saw the relationship between the CUDO and the faculty as uncooperative, neutral, or cooperative. Only 21 percent of AUDOs and a little over 50 percent of CUDOs said cooperative, indicating that the dean at the Central University was not alone in his assessment.

Decentralization helps soften the mistrust. Among the survey respondents, more than 80 percent of AUDOs and 70 percent of CUDOs considered the relationship between the AUDO and the faculty to be cooperative (see figure 22).

One of the major advantages to decentralization is that it encourages and facilitates the direct involvement of the dean and faculty members in the identification and cultivation as well as solicitation of donors. Decentralization creates a broader base of operation and a broader base of support for development activities.

One of the Decentral University deans said that his development

Figure 22. Assessment of Relationship between Development Officers and Faculty

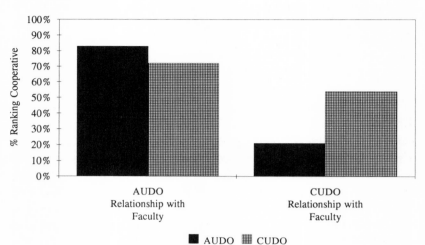

officer was a full participant in the college's programs. She regularly attended college-wide meetings and social events. She served on her share of college committees. She ate in the faculty dining room and was really interested in the research and teaching issues that others brought up in such informal settings. She told faculty about her contacts with prospects to get their reactions to her ideas and plans.

This kind regular collegial contact with the faculty substantially breaks down the stereotypes on both sides. The Decentral University dean said that although the faculty had resisted his initial plans to hire a development officer, they had since become eager to assist with development activities. They offered to have prospective donors serve as guest lecturers where a donor's expertise fit the course topics. They agreed to participate in small seminars where a departmental faculty would meet with a group of prospective donors whose professional interests overlapped with the faculty members' research interests. In this setting, faculty would describe research they were doing and donors would react, question, and comment. Contributions would often result for the department, but also the prospective donors would become more closely affiliated with the college as a whole.

When the development officer is a part of the academic unit, the commonly perceived tension between faculty and fund raisers is ameliorated. By working on school-wide programs such as an MBA case competition or an Engineering Hall of Fame dedication, and by sharing the many group-building experiences of people in close proximity to each other, faculty and fund raisers come to understand each other. The cooperation engendered by this increased understanding advances the goals of each.

The ability of the development officer to succeed in raising money for the school is greatly enhanced by involving the faculty members. They are the people who can really make the case for support to a major donor or a large corporation. The academic unit development officers claimed that faculty were much more willing to work with them than with a central development officer whom they didn't know and who didn't understand their priorities as well as the academic unit development officer.

One of the greatest advantages of a decentralized or hybrid system is that deans have full-time staffing for cultivation activities and a sense of control over the implementation of their fund-raising ideas and plans. This control seemed particularly important to the deans I interviewed. Although some of their colleges' alumni were involved with campus-wide alumni and donor activities, the deans seemed to feel remote from those efforts and eager only to discuss the ones they and their AUDOs had designed and put in place.

Being decentralized or hybrid does not assure that the development officer will be accepted as a full member of the college's leadership group. At Hybrid University, the vice president told me that in some academic units, the development officers had been fully integrated into the management team of the college. In other units they were seen, with more skepticism, as a little outside the mainstream. This depended greatly on the personalities and styles of the development officer and the dean. The vice president encouraged the deans to recognize the development officers as peers of the associate and assistant deans. The more the development officer became a part of the college, the more effective he or she could be in representing the college to both internal audiences and to donors. The development officer who was involved in the full range of college activities would be better able to understand the expertise and the needs of the college and better able to articulate those effectively.

If the dean is going to have the full benefit of a development officer's expertise in implementing the college's academic mission, the development officer must be accepted, trusted, and respected by the faculty. Faculty members tend to value years of experience as well as expertise and productivity. The tenure system creates classes of professionals. Junior, untenured faculty are not peers of senior tenured faculty. Newly minted Ph.D.s may have more expertise than their senior colleagues, but they are not granted senior status until they have worked at the job at least the five or six years necessary to meet minimum tenure standards. And they must prove that they have the respect of their peers at other institutions.

Academic unit development officers are measured by faculty against these standards as well as against administrative standards. The academic unit development officer will be most successful in building a relationship with faculty if he or she meets faculty criteria for being an expert, such as productivity, peer respect, and years of experience. The dean is unlikely to expect the faculty to accept a development officer as a full member of the college's leadership group if that officer has fewer than five years experience, no record of peer recognition, or a soft record of productive solicitation. It may help for a development officer to have advanced degrees and be eligible for an academic title such as assistant or associate dean. On the other hand, if the development officer's degree is in the academic field of the unit, faculty are likely to consider it a sign of weakness for the officer to move out of research and teaching into administration. If the officer's degree is in another academic area, the faculty will consider it inferior and not worthy of serious note. Nevertheless, a degree and a publication and presentation record help indirectly. It will win the development officer peer acclaim, which faculty acknowledge, respect, and demand of their leaders.

The deans at Central University were complimentary of the technical knowledge (particularly about deferred giving plans) of the campus development officers. But they minced few words, indicating their disdain for the development officers' credibility as representatives of the college and its faculty. They said that the central development officers did not understand enough about the college's major instructional programs or the faculty's research to be sent out among the alumni and constituents of the college.

The deans at Decentral University and Hybrid University had similar complaints about the CUDOs but not about their AUDOs. The academic backgrounds of the development officers were similar, most of them having graduated from liberal arts programs.

The deans at Central University believed that they and their faculty were outsiders to the development process. They criticized many aspects of the process that they might not have criticized had they felt more ownership of it.

The decentralized universities seemed to have come closest to overcoming this negative relationship between faculty and fund raisers.

13 | *The Development Officer and the University*

Hɪʀɪɴɢ ᴇꜰꜰᴇᴄᴛɪᴠᴇ ᴅᴇᴠᴇʟᴏᴘᴍᴇɴᴛ ᴏꜰꜰɪᴄᴇʀs is a major concern of the deans and the president. The university needs as many competent, experienced, effective professional development officers as possible. Decentralized, centralized, and hybrid systems have different advantages in the effort to attract and retain good people. At the vice-presidential level, centralized and decentralized systems require more skills than hybrid systems.

The vice president in a decentralized system must have the respect of both the deans and the development officers. Decentralization requires a vice president with advanced interpersonal management skills. The vice president must lead the other senior development people by force of his or her record of past achievement and must create a spirit of university-wide cooperation based on recognition of his or her professional stature. When a conflict arises, the deans and development officers must have confidence that the vice president will propose the best possible alternatives and will mediate with wisdom. A strong vice president can build the team spirit that encourages an academic unit to concede a case.

The vice president for development in a centralized system must possess expertise both in organization and in interpersonal relations. The vice president is responsible for organizing all of the development activities, both operational and functional, for a large institution. The institution may represent thousands of donors and prospective donors, as well as thousands of gifts to be appropriately stewarded. The vice president must also be able to involve the powerful academic leaders of the institution in the development process without conceding to them the authority needed to maintain control of the process. If the vice president is less skilled than necessary, animosity will exist between the deans and the central development office. Their goals differ, since the vice president seeks to raise the maximum amount from each donor for some part of university and the dean seeks to raise the maximum for one part of the university. The president of Central University said he believed that animosity could be minimized by the central development officer if he or she was willing to expend the necessary time to build a friendly relationship with the various deans. However, that will only work if the deans are willing to trust and share.

For example, the deans of business and engineering at Central University said that the advantages to centralization all accrued to the central development office and the disadvantages all accrued to them. One dean mentioned that he was so sure that he could raise more money that he offered to take whatever part of the central development office budget was allocated to his school and whatever development officer the vice president least wanted to keep and guaranteed to double the amount raised within a year. But the vice president "refused to take the offer seriously. He laughed it off. I was hurt."

From the point of view of a senior development officer, however, it is understandable why the vice president would not have taken the offer seriously. Suppose, for example, that the vice president had made such an offer to a dean. Suppose that the development officer, upset because for the fifth time in a year a major donor had called to complain about a student not being able to get a needed class, had offered to manage the assignment of class loads for a year and guaranteed that not one parent or student would complain about a scheduling problem. Although interpersonal skills help in every situation, the centralized development program can call for near-superhuman doses of them.

The hybrid system puts the fewest extraordinary demands on the vice president. Most of the operational and managerial functions are facilitated by having an AUDO with one foot in the central office and the other foot in the academic unit.

In addition to having a strong and effective vice president, a university benefits by having senior professionals in its other development positions. Decentralization creates more opportunity for a university to attract highly skilled development officers for non-vice-presidential positions.

A decentralized structure is particularly attractive to experienced officers who want to lead a program but who are not eager to take on the administrative duties of a vice presidency. The AUDO controls a relatively large program, often as large as the development program of an independent institution. Many academic units have 3000 or more students, 15,000 or more alumni, and faculty of 100 or more. The challenge of leading a development office for this size program is interesting enough to attract an experienced development person.

In addition, the senior academic unit development officer has a built-in group of colleagues with whom to share concerns and successes. He or she does not face the isolation that senior development executives face in independent institutions the same size as the academic unit. Also, some senior development officers resist becoming chief institutional development officers because they do not equate moving up the bureaucratic ladder with professional enhancement. For these development officers, a leadership position with an academic unit is ideal.

Many deans want a senior, rather than a more junior, development officer working with the academic unit. One of the attractions for deans of a fully decentralized system over a hybrid system is that the development officer is more likely to be a senior person. AUDOs in hybrid systems have less freedom than AUDOs in decentralized systems to set an agenda and implement it.

One Decentral University AUDO told me that being a member of the management team of an important component of the university was considerably more rewarding professionally than being a staff officer in the central development office or a member of a hybrid system. It is easier to build relationships with the people who are the heart of the university—the students and the faculty. The priorities of the school are more clear. It is possible to become relatively expert in the areas where the school possesses particular expertise. As a central development officer, there are so many areas of university expertise that it is impossible to try to learn enough to speak in a skillful way about them.

AUDOs become assimilated into the subculture of the unit. This offers advantages when dealing with donors who were also part of that subculture. Humanists do not use the same jargon as engineers. One AUDO claimed that because she had assimilated the unit's jargon and customs, she had better rapport with donors than any central development officer.

The AUDOs at Decentral University said they enjoyed the competition created by a decentralized development system. They learned from each other, they had an extensive peer support system, and they had criteria for evaluating their success without looking outside the institution. They were totally responsible for the advancement of a medium-sized institution while still having colleagues within the wider university.

The Hybrid University AUDOs told me that the action in development is in their colleges. They characterized the central office as a holding company, an administrative branch of the institution. Donors make gifts to support students, faculty, and programs, all of which are located out in the colleges. The Hybrid University AUDOs wanted to be where the action is. They favored decentralization because it put them out in the schools, but they would have liked even more responsibility for designing and implementing their own programs.

One Hybrid University AUDO said he was discouraged from making a long-term commitment because the hybrid system was extraordinarily bureaucratic and, therefore, undermined initiative. A good development officer will be entrepreneurial, will have a sense that he or she is representing the donor to the institution as much as representing the institution to the donor, and will often act as a broker between the institution and the donor. People with these characteristics seldom choose an organization that requires them to report on every activity and conversation with a donor, or to take direction from someone who does not know the donor as well. The hybrid system favors the technocrat over the entrepreneur, according to the AUDO. It forces a development officer to move to another job when he or she becomes more experienced. The largest gifts are managed and controlled by the central development officers.

The development officers in the academic units at Hybrid University considered it to be highly centralized in terms of operations, yet decentralized in the sense that the development officers were dispersed throughout the university. As they saw it, the central office drove and initiated the process of hiring a development officer for a school. The dean had minimal veto power over who was hired. The central office handled most major gift solicitation. The college's development officer was a generalist who worked with midrange donors. The only way to work with major gifts within the system was to take a central job. The AUDOs saw that as a less desirable position because it would force them to relinquish direct contact with the "producers" in the organization.

A former member of the central development staff at Hybrid University pointed out that deans and AUDOs there usually work with prospects in the $100,000 range and lower. The theory is that when the gift is larger than $100,000, the donor will want proposals from more than one college and will want contact with the president and central development officers. Resentment builds among deans and school development officers when they have cultivated a donor until he or she reaches the $100,000 level and then must turn the donor over to the central staff to manage for a big gift.

The Hybrid University vice president addressed this topic from a different viewpoint. He said that when the donor was ready to execute a major gift, the president stepped in to assure the donor that the gift was important to the institution as a whole, not just to one segment of the institution. The vice president believed that donors were pleased to have a combination of academic and administrative attention given to their gifts. Because both the academic and administrative branches were involved in the process, they were more confident that their gift would receive sound fiscal management and would be used to achieve realistic academic goals.

Summary

In summary, centralized and decentralized systems seem to place heavier requirements on the interpersonal and organizational skills of the vice president. Decentralized systems offer the best opportunity for attracting a large number of senior level professional development officers to the university.

14 | *Centralization: Opportunities and Challenges*

A STRONG CENTRAL DEVELOPMENT OFFICE is essential to the well-being of the university as a whole. Some gifts are given primarily in support of academic units, for purposes such as faculty research, curriculum development and enhancement, and assuring diversity among students entering a given field of study. But many gifts continue to be given for university-wide purposes, such as to enable access to higher education for all groups in our society, for library and computer resources, for interdepartmental programs, and for overall enhancement of the university. The sizes of gifts to academic units and to the university as a whole are comparable. The numbers of such gifts are comparable. The value of such gifts to the institution is comparable. The management challenge facing universities is to organize development offices to succeed with both types of gifts. If development is decentralized, who will raise money for university-wide purposes, for interdepartmental projects, and for presidential initiatives? Who will worry about private support for the libraries, or for scholarships, honors programs, and student-affairs projects? Just as the deans need full-time staff to support their fund-raising activities, the president needs strong development leadership to support efforts to enhance the university as a whole. That support includes overseeing all of the university's development activities in order to assure maximum effectiveness and appropriate quality.

Centralized management of development activities enables the university to coordinate and control the cultivation and solicitation of donors more effectively than decentralization allows. A centralized management system can readily provide information on the status of each donor and prospective donor and on the status of each solicitation and gift. It assures that all development activities are under the leadership of an experienced professional development officer. It makes it easier for the university to present alternative proposals from several colleges to a potential donor. It increases the university's ability to present to potential donors those proposals that match the university's highest priorities for funding.

The case study made it clear that the senior development professionals at Central University thought their system had more advantages than disadvantages. The study gave the vice president the authority to meet the responsibilities of the office. The development professionals rejected the idea of a decentralized system in which they would have responsibility for university-wide fund raising but not have the authority or control of resources necessary to assure that an effective and professional development operation was implemented. If resources are being used to support an ineffective development program at a school, the vice president wants to have the means to recapture and redirect those resources.

Centralization has several clear advantages over decentralized and hybrid systems in recruiting and retaining good development officers. Donors' interests are not always wholly tied to the interests of one academic unit. The same potential donor can be involved in the humanities, the fine arts, business, engineering, a medical concern, and athletics. Some donors' interests include a global perspective on the value of diversity of the student body, access for all students, and the teaching of values to college students who will soon become societal leaders. A gift to the university as a whole may be more appropriate for such a donor. The development system of a university should encourage a multiplicity of donor interest and involvement. Segmentation of the development office by decentralization makes reaching this goal difficult.

Senior development officers understand the possibility of multiple donor interests. They enjoy having broad-based as well as high-level responsibility. The advantages of decentralization, which deans praise as attracting senior development officers, become disadvantages if the broad vision of some donors and the broad interests of good development officers cannot be accommodated.

Experienced development officers also value clear communication within an organization. The survey indicated that decentralization does not promote candid communication. Senior development professionals value a system of coordination that protects their efforts with a donor and encourages serious planning of cultivation, solicitation, and stewardship activities. The case study data indicated that the advantages inherent in effective coordination were shared by centralized and hybrid systems but that coordination was more difficult and less effective in a decentralized system.

In centralized systems the development officers are part of the president's staff. Many experienced senior development officers find this an attractive professional environment. They like working at the university level, participating in the management of the larger institution, working with the president and the university's top volunteer board, leading and guiding the overall development program of the institution. For them the centralized system is the most attractive environment.

In contrast, the centralized management system does not provide effective lines of communication and information flow between the academic units and the central development office. It does not provide maximum incentive for all academic unit leaders to effectively participate in development activities. It does not provide staffing for academic unit volunteer boards.

In summary, centralization meets the needs of presidents and vice presidents for development more completely than it meets those of academic deans. A fully centralized system for managing development activities provides effective coordination and control of the development activities. It attracts to top positions the kind of experienced development professionals who enjoy the global perspective offered by working at the presidential level. It provides opportunities for less experienced professionals to learn from seasoned professional development officers and avoids having inexperienced officers reporting to deans who are also without proven development skills. It assigns clearly the responsibilities for development tasks such as major gift solicitations, and it enables clear and effective communication.

On the other hand, centralization of development does not attract senior professionals who are more interested in fund raising itself than in the management of the process. It does not assure effective communication. It requires extraordinary interpersonal skills on the part of the vice president for development. Centralization of the development process does not provide maximum incentive or adequate staffing for deans to be fully involved in fund raising.

The primary advantage of centralization is that it provides strong coordination and control. The primary disadvantage is that it fails to fully involve the deans in the fund-raising process.

15 | *Decentralization: Opportunities and Challenges*

THE PRIMARY ADVANTAGE of decentralization is that it fully involves deans in development activities. The involvement of the deans is increased by giving them full control over development activities for their schools and by allowing each school to fund and manage its own development activities.

The deans of business and engineering at Decentral University, like their president, each indicated that development was one of their three highest priorities, along with articulating the academic mission and recruiting faculty and students.

Decentralized systems encourage deans and faculty members to be directly involved in the identification and cultivation as well as solicitation of donors. They also provide deans with on-the-spot professional guidance and staffing for their development undertakings.

Although the acting president of Central University preferred his system over more decentralized ones, he recognized some specific advantages to decentralization. He believed that a decentralized system captured more of the energy that could be directed to development activities by academic leaders. It also was more effective at "coupling the donor to a program of special interest to him." Since very few donors made large unrestricted gifts, the university needed to tie the donor to a program that he supported or might support. Central development officers were not as effective in creating and maintaining those ties as development officers who were part of the school in which the donor had the most interest. The acting president believed that the number of deans and directors actually involved in visiting prospective donors was lower in a centralized system and that the deans felt less a part of the team. It was essential to have deans involved with development so that the development officers and president were very clear on the school's priorities and expertise.

Decentralization also enables the university to hire a larger number of experienced development professionals because a senior person is needed to head the development program for each of the academic units.

Stewardship is likely to be stronger in a decentralized system. Since the development officer is located in the unit and working daily with the faculty and students of the school, he or she can easily evaluate the impact of the gift and report back to the donor.

When the development officer is a part of the academic unit the commonly perceived tension between faculty and fund raisers is ameliorated.

The fully decentralized system tends not to provide the most effective coordination among various institutional leaders who seek private support. It also does not provide clear lines of communication and information flow between the academic units and the central development office. It is less effective in delineating clear division of responsibilities for development activities. It may not take full advantage of the experience and skill of some of the senior academic unit development officers.

Decentralization of the management of development is appropriate if and only if the rest of the administration of the university is decentralized.

The hybrid system of managing development programs provides effective coordination and control of development activities. It provides clear lines of communication and information flow between the academic units and the central development office. It provides opportunities for all institutional leaders to participate in development activities. It provides some guidelines for the division of responsibilities for development activities.

The deans at Hybrid University generally were more satisfied with the management of development at the institution than they were dissatisfied with it. They described themselves as committed to fund raising and claimed that commitment is absolutely critical to "understanding fund raising policies, procedures, operations and ultimately to being successful." However, the deans interviewed were not in total agreement with each other on the desirability of the system in place.

One dean said he considered it an advantage that little duplication of effort occurs in the hybrid system between what the college's development officer does and what the central development officers do. There is a single strategy for dealing with each donor. More than one development officer is not considering a specific donor at one time. Prospect identification is orderly and prospect management is focused on setting the best plan for each donor given the knowledge of the donor's interests.

The Hybrid University AUDOs concurred that the coordination program worked well. From their point of view, the primary advantage to the hybrid system was its ability to manage prospects and decrease the occurrence of multiple solicitations to individuals and organizational funding sources. The system encouraged open discussion of prospects and their interests. No prospect was assigned without a public discussion and there was no secrecy about prospective donors.

The disadvantage to the system as perceived by the development officers in the colleges was that it was extraordinarily bureaucratic and, therefore, undermined the initiative of its best development officers.

In the hybrid system, academic unit development positions are less attractive to senior officers because they do not provide full leadership to their programs. The system is less attractive than a fully decentralized system to deans and faculty because it is less likely to attract a senior professional to their units.

Summary

In summary, both decentralized and hybrid systems have the advantage of involving the deans fully in the cultivation and solicitation of prospective donors and providing adequate staffing for the deans' fund-raising activities. Both ease the common tensions between development officers and faculty by promoting joint projects and integrating the fund raisers into the college's subculture. They also enhance the stewardship activities by linking donors to specific programs.

Fully decentralized systems have the added advantage of requiring that the deans provide the resources for their fund-raising activities, thereby assuring that the activities will be a chosen priority. Full decentralization encourages deans and development officers to be entrepreneurial and to take initiative, thereby increasing the overall level of fund-raising activity at the university.

In three specific areas, full decentralization has disadvantages that hybrid systems do not have: coordination of prospect management, communication between the academic units and the central development office, and division of responsibility for development tasks.

In contrast to centralized systems, decentralized and hybrid systems, meet the needs of the deans more completely than they meet the needs of CUDOs. The primary advantage of decentralization is that it provides the deans with incentive and staffing for fund raising. The primary disadvantage is that it often fails to provide adequate coordination or control.

16 | *The Dean's Role in Development*

T<small>HE DEANS'</small> <small>LEADERSHIP</small> in development is both pragmatic and philosophical. Pragmatically, the dean must be concerned about how the management structure affects productivity. Three suggestions parallel the three management systems.

If a university chooses to fully centralize its development programs, the deans should encourage the establishment of a deans' development council chaired by the chief university development officer. It should meet regularly to discuss overall strategic and tactical planning. Prospect identification, cultivation, and solicitation should be discussed as well as appropriate stewardship of gifts. Deans should participate in the development planning and should set specific objectives for their units' roles in achieving the goals set for each major prospect.

If a university chooses to establish a fully decentralized system for managing its development programs, the deans should encourage the establishment of both an executive development council and a development committee.

The Executive Development Council and Development Committee would be the core of a development team that would unify the development process of the university without forgoing the advantages of having relatively independent academic unit development offices.

The executive development council would be chaired by the vice president for development and have as its members all senior-level development professionals at the institution. As junior development officers gain quantity and quality of experience, they would be added to the council. The council should set overall university development goals, blending the development goals of the academic units with those that are university-wide, and should make strategic and tactical plans for achieving the goals. The council should give particular attention to setting objectives for achieving university-wide development goals that could not be met by achievement of all academic unit development goals. Particular attention should also be given to setting strategies for involving donors whose interests overlap with more than one component of the university.

The development committee should be chaired by a designee from the staff of the vice president for development. Membership should include all midlevel and novice development officers. The committee should set objectives for the achievement of academic unit and university-wide goals. It should provide guidance, advice, and mentoring for junior development officers as well as assistance with implementation of programs.

Information about academic unit development activities and central office development activities should be shared at both the council and the committee meetings.

If a university establishes a hybrid system for managing its development programs, the deans should establish an active electronic mail program to link themselves and the vice president for development. Regular, informal reports should be exchanged concerning contacts with prospective donors and other development news. The vice president also must share information concerning central office development activities with the academic units and specify clear expectations concerning implementation of programs.

On the philosophical level, a dean is the intellectual and emotional leader of the school's development efforts. The dean must understand and convey the value of philanthropic support to faculty, staff, and students as well as to donors. Major gifts often affect the future direction of a program or even a whole university. Smaller gifts, taken together, provide some greater flexibility in a budgeting process that is otherwise rigid and unable to respond to unexpected opportunities or crises. Smaller gifts from a larger number of donors also counterbalance the potential for a single very large gift to have too great an influence on the priorities of the colleges.

Gifts to higher education show people's loyalty and trust in individual colleges and universities. Giving has a "Tinkerbell factor." When Peter Pan asked us to clap our hands if we believed, through tears of joy and nostalgia, we loudly brought Tink back to life. The annual reports on giving, listing all the donors for the past year, are the applause meters measuring how much people believe in their schools and want them to flourish. Only a few individual gifts can be large enough to make the difference all alone between mediocrity and greatness, but all the gifts, taken together, keep American higher education alive to spread the magic of ideas and wisdom.

Throughout the history of the growth of higher education in America, the relationship between philanthropists and academic leaders has been influential, and it has been important to the survival of colleges and universities. Partnerships between philanthropists with vision and dedicated, wise educators have brought power and freedom to our nation, shaping the structure of postsecondary education. The American system of higher education is the finest in the world because of the diversity and access that it offers to our citizens. Philanthropists assure these strengths. They recognize that even in tight economic times, it is not always wise to eliminate duplication and overlap, to close underutilized facilities, and to consolidate all programs into the strongest ones. Philanthropists assure that a university that is geographically remote and will therefore never have enough students to make some programs cost-effective can still offer them. Philanthropists assure that the disadvantaged student has the financial assistance needed to attend school. Our many and diverse institutions are the building blocks of America's educational force and resilience. It is the legacy of American philanthropists that we have a robust, eclectic, and open system of higher education.

The dean's pragmatic leadership will assure that any of the three systems for managing fund raising will increase the support that the college receives for its work. The dean's philosophical leadership will make clear that gifts to higher education are an investment. The return on philanthropic investment is the transmission to the next generation of the accumulated knowledge of all who came before. It is the chance and hope that future leaders will do an even better job of using that knowledge. The legacy of the partnership between philanthropists and educators is a world that is more wise, more caring, more thoughtful, and more creative.

The dean's reward for accepting leadership for fund raising is the joy of participating in the formation, growth, and productivity of the partnership between wise philanthropists and wise educators.

Appendix 1: | *Survey Questionnaire*

UNIVERSITY DEVELOPMENT SYSTEMS MANAGEMENT SURVEY

1A. Does your university have a development officer whose primary responsibility is fund raising for:

the business school	_____ yes	_____ no
the engineering school	_____ yes	_____ no

If you answered NO to both, please answer 1B, then go directly to question 12.
If you answered YES to either, please skip 1B and proceed.

1B. Do you anticipate having such a development officer within the next two years?
_____ yes _____ no

---

2. To whom do the academic unit development officers report?

	business	engineering
the dean	_____	_____
central development	_____	_____
joint reporting	_____	_____

---

3. Out of which budget are the academic unit development officers paid?

	business	engineering
the dean	_____	_____
central development	_____	_____
joint reporting	_____	_____

---

4. For how long have these positions existed?

	business	engineering
less than 1 year	_____	_____
1 to 3 years	_____	_____
4 to 6 years	_____	_____
7 to 10 years	_____	_____
more than 10 years	_____	_____

---

5. You are the: _____ central development officer
   _____ business development officer
   _____ engineering development officer

---

6. Indicate the number of years of experience each officer has in development:

	Bus DO	Eng DO	Chief DO
0 to 3	_____	_____	_____
4 to 8	_____	_____	_____
9 or more	_____	_____	_____

---

7. How do you rank the skill level of these development officers (DO)?

	Bus DO	Eng DO	Chief DO
senior level	_____	_____	_____
mid level	_____	_____	_____
novice level	_____	_____	_____
not applicable or I don't know	_____	_____	_____

8. How important is **each** of the following in helping the academic unit development officer to successfully plan and execute a development program for the unit?

1 = essential   2 = helpful   3 = unimportant

1	2	3	Being paid by the dean
1	2	3	Reporting to the dean
1	2	3	Being physically located in the academic unit
1	2	3	Being part of the management team of the unit
1	2	3	Having easy access to the dean
1	2	3	Having a high level of interaction with the faculty
1	2	3	Having interaction with students
1	2	3	Interacting with the academic unit's volunteer board
1	2	3	Interacting with the university's primary volunteer board
1	2	3	Having a good rapport with the chief development officer
1	2	3	Having a good rapport with the university president
1	2	3	Having an academic title (Assistant, Associate Dean)
1	2	3	Having a dean who is committed to the development effort

9. The establishement of academic unit development offices has:

_____ tended to increase total philanthropic support reported by the university
_____ tended to decrease total philanthropic support reported by the university
_____ had no significant effect on the university's total philanthropic support

10. How important is the academic unit development officer as a source of information for the dean and academic unit?

about trends and events within the university?

1	2	3	4	5

unimportant   very important

about trends and events outside the university?

1	2	3	4	5

unimportant   very important

11. Check **each** level of gifts which the academic unit development officer manages:

_____ to $1,000   _____ $50,001 to $100,000
_____ $1,000 to $10,000   _____ $100,001 to $1M
_____ $10,001 to $50,000   _____ More than $1M

Begin here if you answered NO to both parts of 1A

12. How important is the central development office as a source of information for the deans and academic units:

about trends and events within the university?

1	2	3	4	5

unimportant   very important

about trends and events outside the university?

1	2	3	4	5

unimportant   very important

13. How would you characterize the relationship between the faculty and the academic unit development office?

1	2	3	4	5

uncooperative   cooperative

between the faculty and the central development office?

1	2	3	4	5

uncooperative   cooperative

14. Has a major gift ever caused a significant shift in the academic priorites of an academic unit?

_____ yes
_____ no

If yes, the solicitation of that gift was managed by:
_____ the academic unit
_____ the central development office
_____ jointly

If yes, the shift in priorities was readily accepted:

by the academic unit:
_____ yes
_____ no

by the central administration:
_____ yes
_____ no

15. How adequate is upward communication from the academic units to the central development officers concerning the planning and execution of development activities for the units—activities such as prospect identification, cultivation, and solicitation?

1	2	3	4	5
inadequate				adequate

16. How adequate is downward communication from the central development officers to the academic units concerning the planning and execution of university development activities?

1	2	3	4	5
inadequate				adequate

17. When the university **IS NOT** in a capital campaign, indicate who you believe should have primary responsibility in each area:

	academic unit	central office	evenly held
annual fund	_____	_____	_____
major individual gifts	_____	_____	_____
major corporate gifts	_____	_____	_____
major foundation gifts	_____	_____	_____
maintaining alumni database	_____	_____	_____
maintaining gift records	_____	_____	_____
prospect identification	_____	_____	_____
case statement preparation	_____	_____	_____
proposal preparation	_____	_____	_____
development priority setting	_____	_____	_____
stewardship of gifts	_____	_____	_____

18. When the university **IS** in a capital campaign, indicate who should have primary reponsibility in each area:

	academic unit	central office	evenly held
annual fund	_____	_____	_____
major individual gifts	_____	_____	_____
major corporate gifts	_____	_____	_____
major foundation gifts	_____	_____	_____
maintaining alumni database	_____	_____	_____
maintaining gift records	_____	_____	_____
prospect identification	_____	_____	_____
case statement preparation	_____	_____	_____
proposal preparation	_____	_____	_____
development priority setting	_____	_____	_____
stewardship of gifts	_____	_____	_____

---

19. For the business and engineering schools, who does each of the following?

	primarily academic unit	primarily central office	evenly held
sets fund raising priorities	____	____	____
prepares the case statement	____	____	____
identifies prospective donors	____	____	____
cultivates interest in supporting the academic unit	____	____	____
orchestrates face-to-face solicitations for major designated gifts, i.e., when to solicit and who will ask	____	____	____
orchestrates face-to-face solicitations for smaller designated gifts	____	____	____
acknowledges designated gifts	____	____	____
assures gifts are used as intended	____	____	____
maintains records of designated gifts	____	____	____
maintains the alumni database	____	____	____
staffs the alumni relations program	____	____	____
staffs public relations program	____	____	____
solicits annual gifts from unit alumni	____	____	____

---

20. Do the academic units have volunteer boards?

	business	engineering
yes	____	____
no	____	____
I don't know	____	____

---

21. How helpful are the volunteer boards with the unit's development efforts?

business   1   2   3   4   5
             not helpful   very helpful

engineering 1   2   3   4   5
             not helpful   very helpful

---

22. At your institution, does a university-wide system exist for:

	yes	no
tracking the cultivation of donors?	____	____
tracking the solicitation of gifts?	____	____
preventing inappropriate multiple solicitations of donors?	____	____

If yes, how effective is the system for:

tracking the cultivation of donors?
1   2   3   4   5
ineffective   effective

tracking the solicitation of donors?
1   2   3   4   5
ineffective   effective

preventing inappropriate multiple solicitations?
1   2   3   4   5
ineffective   effective

23. In your university, does the amount of private support for an academic unit increase the power of its dean:

	among deans?	with the president?
yes	_____	_____
no	_____	_____

24. Indicate the gender of each development officer, if your university has each position:

	female	male
business development officer	_____	_____
engineering development officer	_____	_____
chief university development officer	_____	_____

25. Indicate the salary range of each development officer (DO):

	Bus DO	Eng DO	Chief DO
to $25K	_____	_____	_____
$26K to$40K	_____	_____	_____
$41K to $55K	_____	_____	_____
$56K to $70K	_____	_____	_____
$71K to $85K	_____	_____	_____
$86K to $100K	_____	_____	_____
$101K to $125K	_____	_____	_____
more than $125K	_____	_____	_____
N/A or I don't know	_____	_____	_____

Appendix 2:

Factors in AUDO Success and Division of Responsibilities: Aggregate Results and Comparison Groups

Table A.1: Factors in Success of Academic Unit Development Officers—
Aggregate Responses (in percentages)

Factors	Essential	Helpful	Unimportant
Paid by the dean	21	39	40
Reports to the dean	47	33	21
Located in the unit	58	30	12
Part of management team	66	30	4
Has access to dean	89	10	1
Interacts with faculty	51	47	2
Interacts with students	10	62	28
Interacts with unit's volunteer board	82	16	2
Interacts with university's volunteer board	21	66	14
Has good rapport with CUDO	69	29	1
Has good rapport with president	27	62	11
Has academic title	12	43	45
Has commitment of dean	95	5	0

Note: As elsewhere in the text, all values may not add up to 100 percent.

Table A.2: Factors in Success of Academic Unit Development Officers—Comparison Groups (in percentages)

Factors	CUDOs						AUDOs						Total					
	Decentralized			Hybrid			Decentralized			Hybrid			All CUDOs			All AUDOs		
	E	H	U	E	H	U	E	H	U	E	H	U	E	H	U	E	H	U
Paid by the dean	4	42	54	0	36	67	60	40	0	25	56	19	1	36	63	42	48	10
Reports to the dean	21	46	33	14	42	45	90	10	0	60	33	7	16	43	40	73	23	4
Located in unit	46	42	12	33	42	25	83	17	0	72	21	7	37	42	21	77	22	4
Part of management team	50	42	8	52	43	5	83	13	3	74	23	2	51	42	6	78	19	3
Has access to the dean	79	21	0	88	9	2	90	10	0	93	7	0	85	13	1	92	8	0
Interacts with faculty	50	46	4	47	49	4	47	53	0	58	42	0	48	47	4	53	47	9
Interacts with students	0	58	42	12	51	37	20	60	20	7	77	16	7	54	39	12	70	18
Interacts with unit's volunteer board	96	4	0	91	7	2	72	24	3	74	23	2	93	6	1	73	23	3
Interacts with university's volunteer board	20	64	12	19	65	16	13	70	16	23	63	12	19	66	15	19	66	15
Has good rapport with CUDO	83	17	0	84	14	2	50	47	3	60	40	0	83	15	1	56	42	1
Has good rapport with president	25	54	21	30	51	19	23	70	6	28	67	5	28	52	19	26	59	5
Has academic title	8	33	58	2	30	67	31	48	21	10	57	33	4	31	64	18	53	28
Has commitment of dean	95	5	0	91	6	2	97	3	0	95	5	0	93	6	1	96	4	0

Key: E = essential factor; H = helpful factor; U = unimportant factor; CUDO = chief university development officer; AUDO = academic unit development officer; decentralized = university with decentralized development management system; hybrid = university with hybrid development management system.

Note: As elsewhere in the text, all values may not add up to 100 percent.

Table A.3: Assignment of Primary Responsibility—Aggregate Responses (in percentages)

Tasks	% Responding—Central Office		% Responding—Academic Unit		% Responding—Evenly Held	
	Routine	Campaign	Routine	Campaign	Routine	Campaign
Annual fund	54	59	26	23	20	19
Maintain alumni databases	85	86	4	3	11	11
Maintain gift records	91	89	2	2	6	9
Major individual gifts	43	50	26	17	31	33
Major foundation gifts	49	52	19	13	31	35
Major corporation gifts	42	49	25	14	33	37
Prospect identification	24	30	10	5	66	66
Setting fund-raising priorities	27	35	26	17	47	49
Stewardship of gifts	29	33	23	18	48	49
Case statement preparation	28	42	31	15	41	43
Proposal preparation	16	27	36	24	48	49

Note: As elsewhere in the text, all values may not add up to 100 percent.

Table A.4: Assignment of Primary Responsibility Comparison Groups (in percentages)

Tasks	% Responding—Central Office				% Responding—Academic Unit				% Responding—Evenly Held			
	Routine		Campaign		Routine		Campaign		Routine		Campaign	
	CUDO	AUDO	CUDO	AUDO	CUDO	AUDO	CUDO	AUDO	CUDO	AUDO	CUDO	AUDO
Annual fund	67	38	73	31	14	40	14	41	19	22	14	28
Maintain alumni databases	93	70	94	70	7	43	9	28	27	38	27	45
Maintain gift records	95	83	96	75	0	7	0	4	5	10	4	21
Major individual gifts	64	7	71	13	8	58	4	38	27	35	25	48
Major foundation gifts	66	19	63	26	7	43	9	28	27	38	27	45
Major corporation gifts	60	6	67	16	6	57	3	30	34	37	30	53
Prospect identification	33	8	38	14	2	25	2	10	65	67	60	75
Setting fund-raising priorities	40	2	47	13	8	58	7	34	52	40	46	53
Stewardship of gifts	40	10	43	14	9	46	8	34	51	43	49	52
Case statement preparation	40	10	52	35	17	55	7	24	43	35	40	41
Proposal preparation	22	7	34	13	21	61	13	42	57	18	53	45

Note: As elsewhere in the text, all values may not add up to 100 percent.

Literature Cited

Adams, J. J. 1978. Management of planning. In A. W. Rowland (ed.), *Handbook of Institutional Advancement* (pp. 455–463). San Francisco: Jossey-Bass.

Argyris, C. 1964. *Integrating the Individual and the Organization.* New York: John Wiley & Sons.

Blaney, J. P. 1988. Knowing our place. *Currents.* 14(1):18–21.

Blau, P. M. 1964. *Exchange and Power in Social Life.* New York: John Wiley & Sons.

Council for Aid to Education. 1991. *Voluntary Support of Education 1989–1990.* New York: By the Author.

Curti, M., and Nash, R. 1965. *Philanthropy in the Shaping of American Higher Education.* New Brunswick, N.J.: Rutgers University Press.

Drucker, P. F. 1954. *The Practice of Management.* New York: Harper & Row.

Duronio, M., and Loessin, B. 1991. *Effective Fund Raising.* San Francisco: Jossey-Bass.

Etzioni, A. 1964. *Modern Organizations.* Englewood Cliffs, N.J.: Prentice-Hall.

Franz, P. J., Jr. 1981. Trustees must lead by example. In F. C. Pray (ed.), *Handbook for Educational Fund Raising* (pp. 161–166). San Francisco: Jossey-Bass.

Goldman, R. 1988. Partners at Pomona. *Currents.* 14(1):10–17.

Hofstadter, R., and Metzger, W. 1955. *Academic Freedom in the Age of the College and the University.* New York: Columbia University Press.

Kelly, K. S. 1991. *Fund Raising and Public Relations: A Critical Analysis.* Hillsdale, N.J.: Lawrence Erlbaum Associates, Inc.

Lees, N. C. 1986. Setting the campaign goal. In H. G. Quigg (ed.), *The Successful Capital Campaign* (pp. 129–139). Washington, D.C.: Council for the Advancement and Support of Education.

Likert, R. 1967. *The Human Organization: Its Management and Value.* New York: McGraw-Hill.

Martin, R., and Moore, B. 1985. *Management Structures and Techniques.* Oxford, England: Philip Allan.

McDonald, J. 1950. *Strategy in Poker, Business and War.* New York: W. W. Norton.

Mintzberg, H. 1983. *Power In and Around Organizations.* Englewood Cliffs, N.J.: Prentice-Hall.

Muller, S. 1978. The definition and philosophy of institutional advancement. In A. W. Rowland (ed.), *Handbook of Institutional Advancement* (pp. 1–12). San Francisco: Jossey-Bass.

Odiorne, G. S. 1965. *Management by Objectives.* New York: Pitman.

Literature Cited

Pickett, W. L. 1981. Prerequisites for successful fund raising. In F. C. Pray (Ed.), *Handbook for Educational Fund Raising* (pp. 11–14). San Francisco: Jossey-Bass.

Porter, W. E., ed. 1958. *The Advancement of Understanding and Support of Education.* Washington, D.C.: The American College Public Relations Association.

Pray, F. C. 1981. *Handbook for Educational Fund Raising.* San Francisco: Jossey-Bass.

Reck, W. E. 1946. *Public Relations: A Program for Colleges and Universities.* New York: Harper & Row.

Reichley, R. A. 1978. The alumni movement: An overview. In A. W. Rowland (ed.), *Handbook of Institutional Advancement* (pp. 275–285). San Francisco: Jossey-Bass.

Rowland, A. W. 1974. The management of the institutional advancement program. *College and University Journal,* 13 (2):4–12.

Rudolph, F. 1962. *The American College and University—A History.* New York: Knopf.

Seymour, H. J. 1988. *Designs for Fund-raising.* Ambler, Penn: Fund Raising Institute.

Smith, D. E. 1981. Appropriate goals for giving programs. In F. C. Pray (Ed.), *Handbook for Educational Fund Raising* (pp. 244–249). San Francisco: Jossey-Bass.

Swearer, H. R. 1988. A more perfect union. *Currents.* 14(1):8–9.

Veysey, L. R. 1965. *The Emergence of the American University.* Chicago: University of Chicago Press.